GERMAN MILITARY HANDGUNS, 1879-1918

Arms and Armour Press
LONDON·MELBOURNE

Fortress Publications
ONTARIO

JOHN WALTER

GERMAN MILITARY HANDGUNS, 1879-1918

ERFURT
1893

Published in 1980 by
Arms and Armour Press, Lionel Leventhal Limited,
2-6 Hampstead High Street, London NW3 1QQ
and at 4-12 Tattersalls Lane, Melbourne,
Victoria 3000, Australia.

Published in North America 1980 by
Fortress Publications, Inc., P.O. Box 241,
Stoney Creek, Ontario L8G 3X9, Canada.

British Library Cataloguing in Publication Data:
Walter, John German Military Handguns, 1879-1918.
1. Pistols – Germany – History. 2. Germany – Heer – Firearms.
I. Title. 623.4'43 UD415.G3
ISBN 0-85368-404-9
(Canada: ISBN 0-96904-869-6)

For Sue

Typeset by Ebony Typesetting, Liskeard, England.
Printed by T. & A. Constable Ltd., Edinburgh.
Bound by Hunter & Foulis Ltd., Edinburgh.

CONTENTS

PREFACE & ACKNOWLEDGEMENTS

This book contains detailed — and hopefully accurate — information about the principal German handguns of the Second Reich: the two commission-designed revolvers of 1879 and 1883, the Parabellums of 1904, 1908 and 1913 (LP 08), and the Mauser C 96 taken into emergency service in 1915 alongside blowback personal-defence weapons such as the Langenhan FL-Selbstlader, the Beholla series, the 7.65mm Dreyse and the Walther Modell 4. Fragments of the information have appeared in the guise of articles published in the British periodical *Guns Review* and the American *Gun Collector's Digest*, but the project has since been extensively revised to reflect the latest research.

Part I describes the guns, while Part II is devoted to the cartridges, the complicated and often misunderstood unit markings, the holsters and their makers, and the issue of Parabellums on the outbreak of the First World War.

Content has benefitted greatly from the enthusiastic co-operation of many friends and colleagues, many of whom are experienced authors and researchers in their own right — and could have been forgiven for withholding some of the details they generously supplied! As a result, I would like to acknowledge my special debts to the following:

Dr Rolf Gminder, formerly of Mauser-Jagdwaffen GmbH, whose generosity continues to amaze me: many of the photographs were supplied from his collection — and much came from his (rather than my) efforts.

Major aD Hans-Rudolf von Stein, whose invaluable assistance eliminated many mistakes from the 'issue' chapter. His knowledge meant that information extracted from B. Friedag's *Führer durch Heer und Flotte* could be amended to include units raised between its publication early in 1914 and the outbreak of the First World War.

Joe Schroeder, for supplying several key photographs. He also checked the short chapter devoted to the Mauser C 96.

Reinhard Kornmayer who, in addition to constant encouragement, supplied the bulk of the material on which I based the chapter dealing with the issue of the pistols in August 1914.

Bill Stonley, who kindly read through the manuscript before the final setting was completed. His expertise led to some valuable revisions and the elimination of some embarrassing mistakes.

Per Jensen and Don Bryans, who willingly shared their extensive knowledge of Parabellum holsters and supplied illustrations of specimens in their collections.

Anthony Carter, who supplied copies of the marking regulations of 1909-10.

Karl Schäfer who, unbidden, provided a copy of the original German army manual for the Pistole 08.

Ian Hogg, who read parts of the manuscript and supplied pictures from his photo library.

I also offer my thanks to the following: the Bundesarchiv, D.W. Bailey, W.L. 'Dick' Deibel, Joachim Görtz, Gordon Hughes, Tom Knox, David Penn and the Imperial War Museum, John P. Pearson, Horst Rutsch, Tom Smith, Glen Sweeting , Masami Tokoi, Herb Woodend and the staff of the Pattern Room Collection at RSAF Enfield Lock, and the patent offices in Britain, Germany and the United States of America.

Lastly, I wish to record my gratitude for the continuing support of my publisher, Arms & Armour Press — and in particular, of Anthony Evans, who processed the majority of the maps and line drawings under especially trying conditions.

John Walter
Brighton, 1980.

| Revolvers | **M 1879** | *Nationality:* German. *Other users:* none officially. *Class:* IVd (cartridge revolver, centrefire). *Operating system:* manual. *Adopted:* 21st March 1879. *Obsolescent:* August 1908 (adoption of the Parabellum). *Discarded:* immediately after the First World War. *Manufacturers:* see pages 20-1. |

Features
Locking mechanism: a pawl on the trigger lever locks the cylinder at the instant of firing. *Construction:* solid frame. *Firing mechanism:* single action hammer-lock. *Magazine:* cylinder containing six rounds. *Extractor:* none. *Ejector:* none.
Sights: (front) open barleycorn; (back) fixed V-notch.
Dismantling catch: a spring device retains the cylinder axis pin.
Hold-open: none. *Cocking indicator:* exposed hammer.
Loaded-chamber indicator: none.
Safety devices: a manual 'safety' lever on the rear left side.
Others: a lanyard ring on the butt, a hinged loading gate on the right side of the frame. *Grips:* wood.
Finish: browned, apart from a few blued or greyed parts.

Dimensions
Length overall: 340mm. *Barrel length:* 180mm. *Weight empty:* 1,275-1,290gm. *Rifling:* 6 grooves, right-hand twist. *Pitch:* 1 turn in 572-582mm. *Land width:* 3.71-3.89mm. *Bore diameter:* 10.58-10.69mm. *Groove diameter:* 11.00-11.20mm.

| | **M 1883** | All details as M 1879, except: *Adopted:* 1885? *Length overall:* 270mm. *Barrel length:* 117-120mm. *Weight, empty:* 915-935gm. |

| Parabellum | **P 1908** | *Nationality:* German. *Other users:* (prior to 1918 only) Bulgaria. *Class:* VIc (semi-automatic pistol, centrefire). *Operating system:* short recoil. *Adopted:* 22nd August 1908. *Obsolescent:* February 1940 (adoption of the P 38). *Discarded:* 1945. *Manufacturers:* see page 28. |

Features
Locking mechanism: toggle-joint. *Construction:* the receiver, open-topped and containing the toggle unit, slides back on top of the frame; the toggle opens vertically when the receiver is halted. *Firing mechanism:* striker in breechblock, released by a laterally acting sear.
Magazine: detachable box containing eight rounds.
Extractor: on top of the breechblock.
Ejector: a spring-steel bar on the right side of the receiver.
Sights: (front) open barleycorn; (back) fixed V-notch.
Dismantling catch: on front left side of the frame.
Hold-open: a rising block behind the magazine well of guns made after 1914. *Cocking indicator:* none.
Loaded-chamber indicator: supplementary function of the extractor.
Safety devices: a manual lever on the rear left side of the frame.
Grips: chequered wood. *Finish:* blued, apart from a few parts.
Others: a lanyard loop on the rear of the frame, a stock ridge on the butt-heel of guns made after late 1913 (?).

Dimensions
Length overall: 216mm. *Barrel length:* 100mm. *Weight, empty:* 900-915gm. *Rifling:* 6 grooves, right-hand twist. *Pitch:* 1 turn in 249-254mm. *Land width:* (DWM) 1.85-2.21mm, (Erfurt) 1.83-2.03mm. *Bore diameter:* (DWM) 8.84-8.87mm, (Erfurt) 8.85-8.87mm. *Groove diameter:* (DWM) 9.09-9.12mm, (Erfurt) 9.10-9.13mm.

PART ONE

The Reichsrevolvers of 1879-83

The foundation of the German Empire (Deutsches Reich), in 1871, lead to the amalgamation of the armies of Prussia, Saxony and Württemberg in one consecutively numbered sequence. This meant that all four major armies were placed under unified control, as Wilhelm I of Prussia and Ludwig II of Bavaria had already agreed that control of the latter's army would pass to the former in the event of war or grave national emergency – the result of a treaty signed in Versailles on 23rd November 1870[1]. The Prussian, Saxon and Württembergian detachments of the Imperial Army (Reichsheer) were ultimately clothed in similar uniforms, and standard weapons were required to complete uniformity. However, the Bavarians pursued an independent line in weapons and equipment into the 1880s, and several years sometimes elapsed between the adoption of a 'standard' weapon in the rest of the Empire and in Bavaria. The single-shot M 1869 ('Werder') breech-loading rifles, which had been issued in small numbers during the Franco-Prussian War, were retained by the Bavarian army throughout the 1870s, for example – at a time when the other states were exchanging their Dreyse needle rifles and an assortment of percussion-ignition rifle muskets for the new Mauser bolt-action breech-loaders.

The Mauser was finally adopted on 22nd March 1872[2] as the 'Infanterie-Gewehr Modell 1871' and represented the first step towards uniformity. And once the design of the long-arms had been finalised, development work began on hand-guns. The Prussian troops were then carrying obsolete single shot muzzle-loading M 1850 percussion-ignition pistols, while small quantities of a Werder system dropping-block cartridge pistol, the M 1869, were seeing service in Bavaria. Some Saxons carried copies of a Smith & Wesson revolver[3], while Württemberg infantrymen relied on a motley collection of muzzle-loaders.

After the Austro-Prussian, or Seven Weeks' War of 1866, many officers had purchased non-regulation revolvers such as the British Adams and American Colt. In addition, many Prussian troops had carried copies of the Beaumont-Adams, made in Suhl, during the Franco-Prussian War. The navy, with its smaller complement, could afford to arm its men with better weapons than those issued to the poor and often abused infantry, as the total expenditure involved was relatively small.

Revolver M79
Various makers

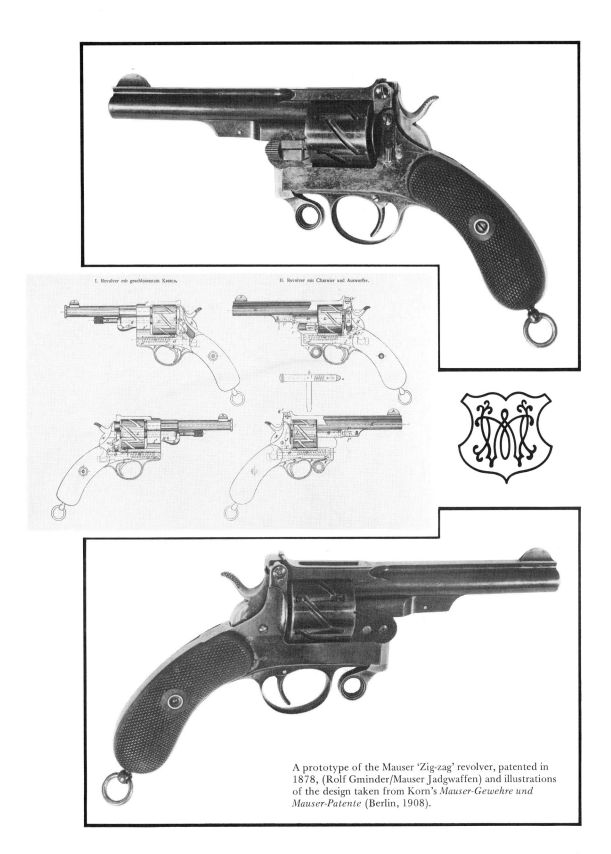

I. Revolver mit geschlossenem Kasten.   II. Revolver mit Charnier und Auswerfer.

A prototype of the Mauser 'Zig-zag' revolver, patented in 1878, (Rolf Gminder/Mauser Jadgwaffen) and illustrations of the design taken from Korn's *Mauser-Gewehre und Mauser-Patente* (Berlin, 1908).

In 1877-8, a committee convened in the government arsenal at Spandau to consider contemporary revolver technology. Apart from the few naval service revolvers, limited manufacture of Lefaucheux-type pinfires by companies such as Schilling of Suhl and Fischer of Lübeck, and copies of Smith & Wesson Russian Model revolvers being made in Berlin by Ludwig Loewe & Co.[4], the board was handicapped by inexperience. Many foreign designs were examined in considerable detail, but the Germans had never contemplated large-scale issues of revolvers and found it difficult to assess the merits of the latest contemporary advances. They were also handicapped by their basic conservatism — which was shared with most other armies of the time. Some of the revolvers they examined were insufficiently robust, while others possessed bizarre features or weird ammunition; and though a few were of highly advanced and efficient construction the trial board's caution only succeeded in producing a weapon that was obsolescent before it was introduced — certainly when judged by contemporary Smith & Wesson standards.

The Modell 1879 revolver was adopted on 21st March 1879 in preference to its competitors. It is now widely known as the 'Reichs-Revolver' or (incorrectly) as the 'Reichs-Commissions-Revolver' in honour of its parentage; its other synonyms include 'Deutsches Armee-Revolver M 79', 'Armee-Revolver, langer Lauf' and many others. The date designations were used officially, however, and are used here. The Loewe-made Smith & Wesson Russian Model copy was one of the best of the M 1879's rivals, but the trial board pursued simplicity to extremes and rejected any unusual, complicated or additional features: latch locks, for example, were viewed with suspicion on the grounds that they could work loose and endanger the firer — even though most break-action revolvers were specifically designed to avoid this problem. In many cases, the hammer could not reach the chambered cartridge until a half-open latch had been forced shut by the hammer blow. It was also argued, with perhaps rather more truth, that the frames of break-action revolvers were generally weaker than those of solid-frame designs. Most of the revolvers that had been adopted by European armies were, after all, solid-frame patterns.

All extraction and ejection systems, including under-barrel rods and automatic ejectors, were abandoned — until the final 'Reichs-Revolver' relied on nothing more sophisticated than a removable cylinder and a separately carried ejecting rod.

Many contemporary military authorities believed that revolvers — and magazine rifles, for that matter — were wasteful of ammunition, and anything that speeded loading, and, therefore, the potential waste of ammunition, was frowned on still more. Ian Hogg[5] says of the lack of an extraction/ejection system: *. . . it may well have been that the commission subscribed to the contemporary theory that it was the duty of officers and NCOs to supervise the activities of the soldiers and not get themselves embroiled in personal combat. Therefore, since the revolvers would only be used for one or two desperate shots when things got out of hand, rapid reloading was a luxury. . .*

It has also been suggested that the absence of an extraction/ejection system resulted from existing patent legislation, but this is unlikely: the rifle committee of 1887-8, which designed the hybrid Gewehr 88, initially paid no attention to infringements of Mauser and Mannlicher patents[6].

Above: *the commission-designed revolver cylinder, showing the recessed-head chambers and the cylinder indexing block (Ian Hogg). Two contemporary*

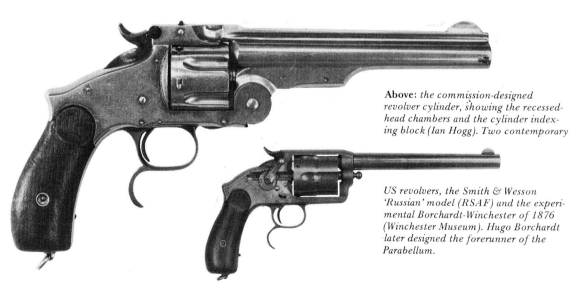

US revolvers, the Smith & Wesson 'Russian' model (RSAF) and the experimental Borchardt-Winchester of 1876 (Winchester Museum). Hugo Borchardt later designed the forerunner of the Parabellum.

The M 1879 revolver was conceived as a cavalry weapon, and the well known difficulties of reloading a revolver on horseback probably accounted for its simplicity. The first issues of the guns and their holsters, the Revolvertasche M 1881, were made to the dragoons on 31st August 1881 — at a time when cavalry still performed its traditional role: a charge, a mêlée, and a rapid withdrawal to regroup. Six shots were adequate for the short time in which a cavalryman was engaging the enemy, and his sabre or broadsword was still regarded as his principal weapon. Loading the revolver could be undertaken while awaiting the next charge.

Subsequent issues of the M 1879 were made to the cuirassiers (Kürassiere) from 1st February 1883, and to officers, NCOs, standard bearers and musicians of the infantry (Offiziere, Unteroffiziere, Fahnenträger and Regiments-Tambours). This occurred prior to the advent of field equipment orders, or Feldausrüstungsordre, in 1885. The revolver is not described, but, for reasons that follow, is assumed to be the M 1879 rather than the 'M 1883'. On 24th February 1887, use of the M 1879 was extended to personnel of the horsedrawn artillery, replacing their Pistolen M 1850. The first official mention of the Revolver M 1883 does not occur until 1891[7], which means that all pre-1890 references to 'a revolver' probably concern the M 1879.

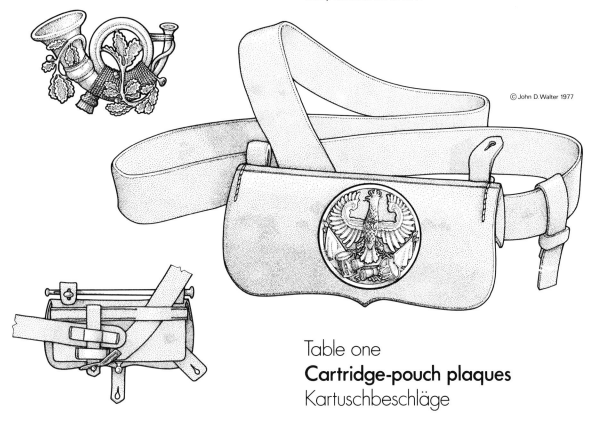

© John D. Walter 1977

Table one
Cartridge-pouch plaques
Kartuschbeschläge

The revolver-armed non-commissioned officers were issued with a cartridge pouch (Kartusche) containing eighteen rounds. This item was adopted on 31st August 1881 — on the same day as the standard holster — and may be found with a decorative plaque attached to the pouch-flap.

All Kartuschen M 81 were made of black leather, except those issued to the Jäger zu Pferde and the Marine-Feld-Batterie — which were brown.

Gardes du Corps

Gardes du Corps — a silver-plated 'Gardestern' (Guard Star), eight-pointed with a central motif of a displayed eagle and the motto 'Suum Cuique'.

Cuirassiers/Kürassiere

Garde-Kürassier-Regiment — a brass Gardestern.
Leib-Kürassier-Regiment Grosser Kurfürst (Schlesisches) Nr. 1 — a displayed eagle clasping a sword and a sheaf of thunderbolts, below the motto 'Pro Gloria et Patria' on a scroll.

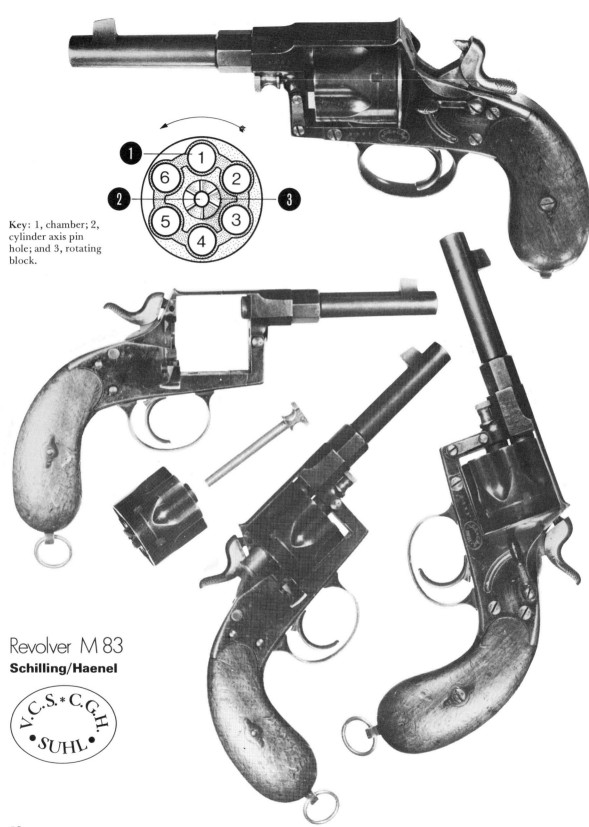

Key: 1, chamber; 2, cylinder axis pin hole; and 3, rotating block.

Revolver M 83

Schilling/Haenel

V.C.S. * C.G.H.
• SUHL •

Kürassier-Regiment Königin (Pommersches) Nr. 2 — *a displayed eagle with an 'FR' cypher on its breast, clasping a sceptre and an orb, atop a trophy of arms and flanked by two enflamed grenades.* Kürassier-Regiment Graf Wrangel (Ostpreussisches) Nr.3; Kürassier-Regiment von Driesen (Westfälisches) Nr. 4; Kürassier-Regiment Herzog Friedrich Eugen von Württemberg (Westpreussisches) Nr.5; Kürassier-Regiment Kaiser Nikolas I von Russland (Brandenburgisches) Nr.6; Kürassier-Regiment von Seydlitz (Magdeburgisches) Nr.7; and Kürassier-Regiment Graf Gessler (Rheinisches) Nr.8 — *as Leib-Kürassier-Regiment but without the flanking grenades.*

Dragoons/Dragoner

1. Garde-Dragoner-Regiment Königin Viktoria von Grossbrittanien und Irland — *a brass Gardestern.*
2. Garde-Dragoner-Regiment Kaiserin Alexandra von Russland — *a German silver Gardestern.*
Grenadier-Regiment zu Pferde Freiherr von Derfflinger Nr.3 (despite its title, still a dragoon unit) — *a brass Gardestern, with an enflamed grenade at each of the four corners of the pouch-flap.*
Dragoner-Regiment Prinz Ulbricht von Preussen (Littauisches) Nr. 1;
1. Brandenburgisches Dragoner-Regiment Nr.2 — *a displayed eagle with the cypher 'FR' on its breast, atop a trophy of arms.*
Dragoner-Regiment von Bredow (1.Schlesisches) Nr.4; Dragoner-Regiment Freiherr von Manteuffel (Rheinisches) Nr.5; Magdeburgisches Dragoner-Regiment Nr.6; Westfälisches Dragoner-Regiment Nr.7; Dragoner-Regiment König Friedrich III (2.Schlesisches) Nr.8; Dragoner-Regiment König Karl I von Rumänien (1.Hannoversches) Nr.9; Dragoner-Regiment König Albert von Sachsen (Ostpreussisches) Nr.10; Dragoner-Regiment von Wedel (Pommersches) Nr.11; Dragoner-Regiment von Arnim (2.Brandenburgisches) Nr.12; Schleswig-Holstein'sches Dragoner-Regiment Nr.13; Kurmärkisches Dragoner-Regiment Nr. 14; 3.Schlesisches Dragoner-Regiment Nr.15; and 2.Hannoversches Dragoner-Regiment Nr.16 — *a displayed eagle with the cypher 'FR' on its breast, atop a trophy of arms.*
1.Grossherzoglich Mecklenburgisches Dragoner-Regiment Nr. 17;
2.Grossherzoglich Mecklenburgisches Dragoner-Regiment Nr. 18 — *a brass star bearing the arms of Mecklenburg-Schwerin.*
Oldenburgisches Dragoner-Regiment Nr. 19 — *a displayed eagle with the cypher 'FR' on its breast, atop a trophy of arms.*
1. Badisches Leib-Dragoner-Regiment Nr. 20; 2. Badisches Leib-Dragoner-Regiment Nr.21; 3. Badisches Leib-Dragoner-Regiment Nr.22 — *a brass plaque displaying the Baden rampant griffin.*
Garde-Dragoner-Regiment (1.Grossherzoglich Hessisches) Nr.23;
Leib-Dragoner-Regiment (2.Grossherzoglich Hessisches) Nr. 24 — *a crowned gothic 'L' cypher, for Grossherzog Ludwig IV, in brass.*
Dragoner-Regiment Königin Olga (1. Württembergisches) Nr. 25 — *none.*
Dragoner-Regiment König (2.Württembergisches) Nr. 26 — *the 'Star of the Order of the Württemberg Crown' in German silver.*

Hussars/Husaren

Leib-Garde-Husaren-Regiment — *a brass Gardestern.*
1. Leib-Husaren-Regiment — *a German silver Gardestern.*
2. Leib-Husaren-Regiment — *a brass Gardestern.*
Braunschweigisches Husaren-Regiment Nr. 17 — *a brass star with a crowned 'W' cypher and the motto 'Immota Fides'.*
Husaren-Regiment König Albert (1.königlich Sächsisches) Nr. 18;
Husaren-Regiment (2.königlich Sächsisches) Nr. 19 — *a crowned and enwreathed Saxon arms, in brass.*
No other hussar regiments were granted plaques.

TABLE ONE **2**

Lancers/Ulanen

1. Garde-Ulanen-Regiment — *a German silver Gardestern.*
2. Garde-Ulanen-Regiment — *a brass Gardestern.*
3. Garde-Ulanen-Regiment — *a German silver Gardestern.*
Königs-Ulanen-Regiment (1.Hannoversches) Nr. 13 — *a crowned 'WR II' cypher, in brass.*
1. Ulanen-Regiment Kaiser Franz-Josef von Österreich-Ungarn (1. königlich Sächsisches) Nr.17; Ulanen-Regiment (2.königlich Sächsisches) Nr. 18; Ulanen-Regiment Kaiser Wilhelm II, König von Preussen (3.königlich Sächsisches) Nr. 21 — *a crowned and enwreathed Saxon arms, in brass.*
No other lancer regiments were granted plaques.

Mounted riflemen/Jäger zu Pferde

Regiment Königs-Jäger zu Pferde Nr. 1 — *a crowned bugle-and-oakleaves and a 'WR II' cypher, in brass.*
Jäger-Regiment zu Pferde Nr. 2 to Nr. 6 — *a bugle-and-oakleaves, in brass.*
Jäger-Regiment zu Pferde Nr. 7 to Nr. 13 carried the Patronen-tasche 01 on the belt rather than the Kartusche 81.
Garde-Reiter-Regiment (Saxony), Karabiner-Regiment (Saxony) — *a crowned and enwreathed Saxon arms, in brass.*
Bavarian cavalrymen were not granted decorative plaques.

Field artillery/Feldartillerie

Prussian regiments (Garde 1-4 ; ordinary, 1-11, 14-24, 26-7, 30-1, 33-47, 50-9, 62-3, 66-7, 69-76) — *a triple-enflamed grenade charged with the cypher 'FWR', in brass.*
Mecklenburg-Schwerin unit (60) — *as above, but with the 'FF' cypher of Grossherzog Friedrich-Franz.*
Mecklenburg-Strelitz contingent (third battalion of Holstein'sches Feldartillerie-Regiment Nr. 24) — *as above, but with the 'FW' cypher of Grossherzog Friedrich-Wilhelm.*
Hessen units (26,61) — *two cannon barrels in saltire above a pyramid of six cannon balls, in brass.*
Württemberg units (13, 29, 49, 65) — *an enflamed brass grenade bearing the cypher 'KR'.*
Saxon units (12, 28, 32, 48, 64, 68, 77-8) — *a crowned and enwreathed Saxon arms, in brass.*
Bavarian regiments (1-12) — *two brass cannon barrels in saltire.*

Train & miscellaneous

Garde-Train-Bataillon — *a brass Gardestern.*
Grossherzoglich Hessisches Train-Bataillon Nr. 18 — *a brass crowned gothic 'L' cypher.*
Train-Bataillon (1.königlich Sächsisches) Nr. 12; Train-Bataillon (2. königlich Sächsisches) Nr. 19 — *a crowned and enwreathed Saxon arms, in brass.*
Prussian and Bavarian train battalions were not awarded plaques.

Special units

TABLE ONE 3

Marine-Feld-Batterie, Tsingtao — *an imperial crown in brass.*

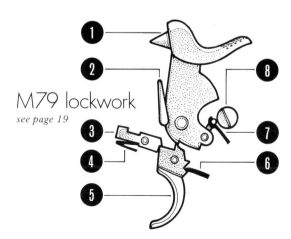

M79 lockwork
see page 19

The M 1879 is a solid, dependable and reliable single-action design with few unusual or advanced features. One writer at least has stated that its trigger mechanism was based on that of the French Mle 1873, the so-called 'Chamelot-Delvigne', but this theory is not wholly satisfactory. The barrel carried an integral front sight and was screwed tightly into an octagonal extension of the frame, while the conventional partly-fluted cylinder was retained by a radial spring-lever on the left side of the frame body. The transverse nose of the lever intercepted and locked the cylinder axis pin. Most springs simply rested against a flat surface, but were retained by a detent in the form of a small protrusion on the spring-lever knob. A few — probably commercial variations — have been reported with the spring-lever inset in the frame, so that it had to be pulled out before it could be rotated. The combination of the spring and the lever was one of the revolvers' bad features, since the former often broke if the unit was turned downwards through greater than 90°. The later M 1883 rectified the fault, but in its own slightly odd way.

M 1879 revolvers all had safety levers on the left rear of their frames, below the hammer, which rotated downwards to prevent the hammer body moving back through the cutaway lever spindle. The usefulness of this device, which is rarely found on other revolvers, is questionable; it cannot be applied at full-cock, but only at half-cock or with the hammer down on the chamber. The hammer can still be dropped from half-cock simply by pulling the trigger, and though this rarely fired the original German service cartridges (which were suitably insensitive) it is still potentially dangerous. A good blow on the hammer, once it has been released from half-cock, will unquestionably fire the gun.

The cylinder held up to six rounds, each being inserted individually through a laterally swinging gate on the right rear of the frame. Each chamber was recessed for the case rim and the cartridges were, consequently, completely encased in metal. There was no gap between the rear face of the cylinder and the standing frame, a characteristic of most other revolvers. The encased-head safety feature has since been 'introduced' several times, on each being hailed as a new development[8]. Spent cases or unwanted rounds could only be removed by punching them out, unless the cylinder was removed from the frame. A separate ejecting rod, carried on the outside of the accompanying cartridge box, was normally used to push each spent case backwards and out through the loading gate.

Service revolvers, apparently without exception, had their chambers numbered from 1 to 6 on the cylinder surface. This feature has been explained in several ways, the most popular being that it told the firer — assuming he had started with the hammer on chamber one — how many rounds he had left. This eliminated one of the worst faults of a revolver, in which the cartridges are hidden from view and in whose design there is rarely a way of marking an empty magazine[9]. An alternative theory has been advanced by Chamberlain[10], who has stated: *The chambers of military revolvers and many of the civilian specimens were numbered clockwise 1 through 6. There is a good, military, reason for this: range safety. The firer loaded chambers 5 through 1 at a loading table under the supervision of a junior NCO. The revolver would then be at half-cock, the cylinder bolt free. The firer would then ease the hammer off half-cock and lower it so that the fixed hammer nose rested in the empty number 6 chamber, which would automatically be in that position if the firer had begun with number 5. . . . The firer would then reapply the safety catch, locking the hammer, and proceeded to the firing point when commanded. . .*

This may not have been the primary function of the marks which, after all, are on a military rather than practice weapon; it may, however, have been a useful by-product. The half-cock position disengaged the cylinder-lock pawl ('cylinder bolt') and permitted the cylinder to turn freely on its axis, giving easy access to the chambers for loading or unloading.

GEBR. MAUSER & CIE.
1880
OBERNDORF

A typical single-action M 1879 revolver, made by Gebrüder Mauser & Co. in 1880 and issued to the Württemberg army in 1882 (W.H.J. Chamberlain collection). **Inset:** *Peter-Paul and Wilhelm Mauser, founders of the company (Mauser-Jagdwaffen GmbH).*

The first contracts for the M 1879 revolver were placed with private manufacturers in Oberndorf, Sömmerda and Suhl. The few made in Oberndorf were delivered to the Royal Württemberg army by Gebrüder Mauser & Co., who had unsuccessfully entered the C/78 break-action and solid-frame revolvers in the original trials. The quantities concerned were very small, as perhaps less than 4,500 were made between 1880 and 1882-3: but then Württemberg's army was small, compared to that of Prussia. Gebrüder Mauser & Co. became Waffenfabrik Mauser AG in April 1884, but no guns have been examined with the later company marks.

Guns made in Sömmerda were the work of Waffenfabrik Franz von Dreyse, owned by the son of the inventor of the famous needle rifle, and most were consigned to the Prussian army. Production in Suhl was initially entrusted to a combine of V.C. Schilling, C.G. Haenel and Spangenberg & Sauer[11], whose mark consisted of S. & S. V.C.S. C.G.H. SUHL in an oval cartouche. Most of these went to Prussia and Saxony.

Very few M 1879 revolvers have been reported with Bavarian markings, apart from those applied by units raised in the First World War, and it is clear that the single-shot M 1869 pistols served until the 1890s. The M 1883 may well have been the first revolver to be issued in large numbers to Bavarian servicemen. No revolvers have yet been examined with the AMBERG mark of the state arsenal.

Most weapons bore the company markings — ● GEBR. MAUSER & CIE. OBERNDORF ● , for example — in a cartouche on the left side of the frame, below the cylinder. The serial numbers appeared on the frame in front of the maker's mark, on the side of the octagonal barrel extension, on the left side of the octagonal part of the barrel where it screwed into the frame, on the front of the loading gate, and on the rear face of the cylinder. The numbers rarely had letter prefixes or suffixes.

Additional marks such as '10,55' (varying between 10,50 and 10,80), struck into the top left flat of the barrel octagon, represented the true rather than nominal calibre. An issue date, which is sometimes difficult to distinguish from the date of manufacture, may appear on the front lower left side of the frame, and there were often inspection and unit stamps as well. The last two digits of the serial number were repeated on most of the removable parts — including the several screws — as complete interchangeability was rarely achieved.

The revolvers were browned overall, except for the grey-pickled hammer and trigger and blued external fittings such as the safety lever, the cylinder axis pin and the axis-pin catch. The M 1879 was accompanied by a leather holster, designated the 'Revolvertasche M 1881' — except in Bavaria[12] where it was the 'M 1882'. Several different types of this holster have been noted, depending on whether they were intended for infantry or mounted units.

The M 1879 revolver, like the M 1883, was extensively used during the First World War. Although nominally replaced by the Parabellum, which had entered service in mid 1909, many thousands of old guns had been stored for the Landwehr and other units raised only on general mobilisation. When hostilities began in 1914, these were taken out of their storerooms, refurbished and issued to Landwehr, second-line, lines of communication and depot personnel. Many revolvers have been examined with the marks of munitions columns and auxiliary units raised during the war.

Typical revolver markings

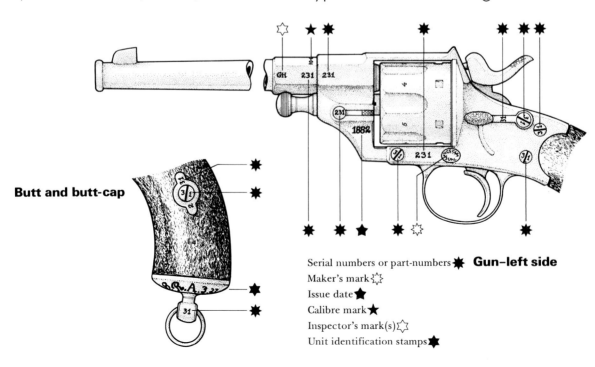

Butt and butt-cap

Serial numbers or part-numbers ✳   **Gun–left side**
Maker's mark ☆
Issue date ★
Calibre mark ★
Inspector's mark(s) ☆
Unit identification stamps ✳

Revolver Modell 1879

The gun and its accessories

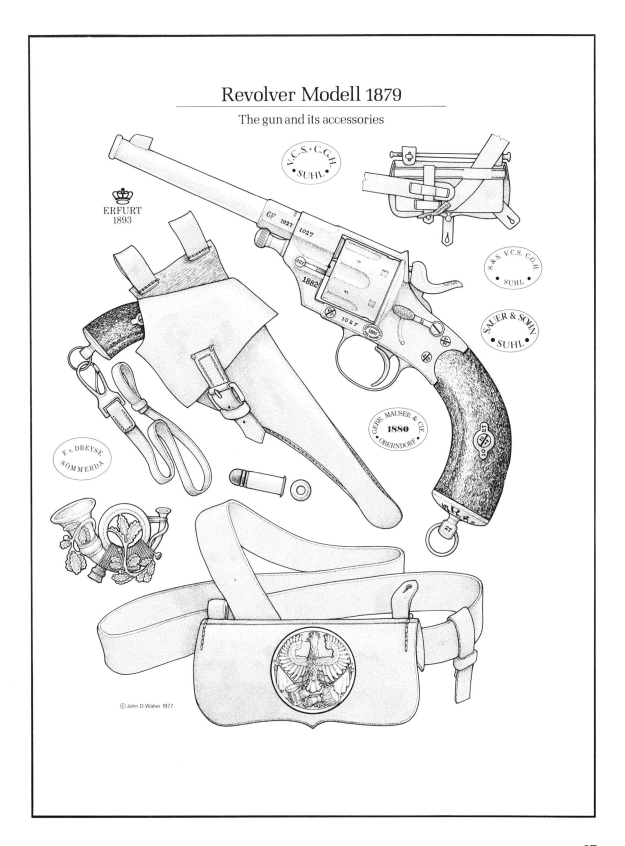

V.C.S. ∗ C.G.H. • SUHL

ERFURT 1893

S. & S. V.C.S. C.G.H. • SUHL

SAUER & SOHN • SUHL

GEBR. MAUSER & CIE 1880 • OBERNDORF

F. v. DREYSE SÖMMERDA

© John D. Walter 1977

The so-called M 1883 revolver was little more than a minor variant of the M 1879. It may originally have been conceived in the early 1880s to arm officers, NCOs, standard bearers and musicians of the infantry regiments, but the only order that could be traced (dating from 1885) simply specifies 'a revolver', without giving details of the model designation. It seems likely that this still referred to the M 1879, because *no* model date was specified; it seems logical to conclude that only one pattern was then being issued, otherwise a distinction would have been made. On 12th March 1891, however, the M 1883 was issued to dismounted personnel of the mobile artillery batteries (fahrenden Artillerie-Batterien). The accompanying holster was introduced as the Revolvertasche M 1891 (called the 'M 1892' in Bavaria), which supports a suggestion that issues of the M 1883, regardless of when it was developed, did not begin until the early 1890s; in addition, a survey of small numbers of dated M 1883 revolvers revealed that few were made before 1893. Most of these weapons were the products of the government arsenal in Erfurt, as the majority of the guns made by private contractors bore nothing other than — in a few isolated cases — issue dates. Some 'contract' guns also bore the proof marks introduced by the 1891 proof law, which was not implemented until 1893[13], but as most contract-made guns bear little more than the maker's mark, evidence based purely on dated government-made specimens must be treated as purely circumstantial.

The lock work of the single-action M 1883 greatly resembled that of its predecessor, the M 1879. Its barrel, however, was noticeably shorter and lacked the muzzle reinforcement (Mundungswüst), though a few hybrids now exist with M 1883 frames and 'long' M 1879 barrels. The frame extension and the breech end of the barrel remained octagonal. The butts of military M 1883 revolvers were more sharply curved than the earlier design; and the cylinder axis-pin retainer, formerly a radial spring-lever, consisted of a vertical leaf spring and a press-catch. This was intended to eliminate the parts breakages that had been common among the older revolvers. All standard M 1883 weapons had plain trigger guards, lanyard rings on the butts, and much the same marks — except for different makers' stamps — as their predecessors.

Many of the companies that made revolvers to army contracts also accepted private orders — from officers, for example, who were allowed to purchase their own guns. Many such revolvers were specially finished; some had chequered wooden or rubber grips, and some even had double-action lock work. These special guns could be distinguished by the position of the trigger within the trigger guard, as it was set well forward to permit the longer double-action 'pull'.

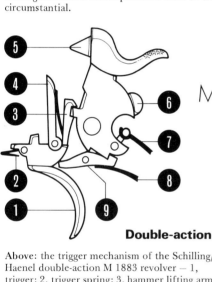

M 1883

Double-action

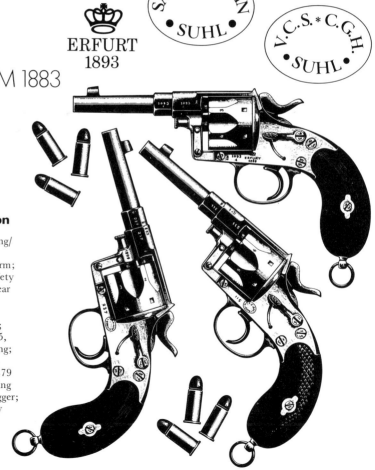

ERFURT 1893

SAUER & SOHN • SUHL •

V.C.S. * C.G.H. • SUHL •

Above: the trigger mechanism of the Schilling/Haenel double-action M 1883 revolver — 1, trigger; 2, trigger spring; 3, hammer lifting arm; 4, cylinder indexing pawl; 5, hammer; 6, safety lever spindle; 7, mainspring; 8 sear, and 9, sear spring. **Opposite right**: the Dreyse double-trigger system. *Key* — 1 front trigger and cylinder-locking-bolt spring; 2, front trigger; 3, cylinder lock; 4, cylinder indexing pawl; 5, hammer; 6, safety lever spindle; 7, mainspring; 8, rear trigger spring; 9, rear trigger; and 10, hammer lifting arm. **Opposite left**: the M 1879 action. *Key* — 1, hammer; 2, cylinder indexing pawl; 3, cylinder lock; 4, spring for 3; 5, trigger; 6, trigger spring; 7, mainspring; and 8, safety lever spindle.

Small numbers of double trigger M 1883-type revolvers were made by Waffenfabrik von Dreyse, although they were otherwise much the same as the service weapons. The unusual mechanism was probably patented or registered in Germany; however, relevant papers have yet to be found. In some respects, the Dreyse system resembles those pioneered some years earlier in the British Tranter revolvers[14], which had additional 'spur-triggers' to cock the firing mechanism before the true trigger tripped the hammer: combining, in effect, single and double action. The advantages of trigger-cocking the action for single-action fire, without thumbing back the hammer, were negated by needless complication.

Dreyse may have made as many as three thousand double trigger revolvers, probably in the period 1892-4/5, as well as standard M 1879 and M 1883 service weapons. However, the several double trigger revolvers available for study are all numbered between 2500 and 2700, and it may be that production was confined to a few hundred in the 2000-3000 range. Too few have been examined to establish this. Apart from the distinctive trigger layout, these revolvers have ugly spurred trigger guards of the type often found on German sporting rifles but were nevertheless built on standard M 1883 frames. At least one gun, number 2634[15], has an under-barrel spring-loaded rod ejector. (The rod may not be contemporary with the gun, however.) It is not clear whether Dreyse, having made substantial numbers of standard weapons, suddenly realised that such a device was a useful addition — especially if the regulation ejecting rod was not carried.

Many M 1883 revolvers saw widespread second-line service during the First World War. Others, based on the M 1883 action, were made in Liége with under-barrel rod ejectors much like those of some early Colt cartridge revolvers. Most of the Belgian copies, which are thought to have been made by Auguste Francotte & Cie, were distributed through commercial channels. None was bought by the German armies.

Dreyse system

Dreyse revolvers

F. v. DREYSE SÖMMERDA

M 79 single-action

Table two **Reichsrevolver manufacturers**

Gebrüder Mauser & Companie. Oberndorf am Neckar, Württemberg. This company was founded by the brothers Peter-Paul (1838-1914) and Wilhelm (1834-1882) Mauser in 1872. Their Oberndorf workshop was destroyed by fire in 1874, but the government firearms factory in Oberndorf was acquired in the same year, the name changed to 'Gebrüder Mauser & Cie', and trading continued. On 1st April 1884, stock was issued and the name changed to 'Waffenfabrik Mauser AG'. This in turn changed to 'Mauser-Werke AG' in 1922. Small numbers of M 1879 revolvers are known to have been made between 1880 and about 1883, as none has been reported with 'Waffenfabrik Mauser' markings.

S

Waffenfabrik von Dreyse, Sömmerda. This concern was founded in 1842 (?) by Johann Niklaus von Dreyse (1787-1867), the inventor of the bolt-action needle rifle, to succeed a business called 'Dreyse & Collenbusch'. Revolvers were made from 1892 until about 1895 under the initial supervision of Franz von Dreyse (c.1819-94), the son of the founder. After his death, the business steadily deteriorated and was acquired by Rheinische Metallwaren- und Maschinenfabrik (later Rheinmetall AG) in 1901.

S, Dr

V.C. Schilling & Companie, Suhl. This metalworking company is known to have been making muskets and rifles as early as the mid nineteenth century, and continued to make shotguns, pistols, rifles and revolvers until the end of the First World War. M 1879 revolvers were made in collaboration with C.G. Haenel and Spangenberg & Sauer, the combine trading as the 'Handfeuerwaffenfabrik-Genössenschaft, Suhl' until Spangenberg & Sauer left the group in the mid 1880s. Schilling the continued to make revolvers in a loose partnership with Haenel. The company was acquired by Heinrich Krieghoff Waffenfabrik, of Suhl, in 1904.

S, Da

C.G. Haenel & Companie, Suhl. This company was one of a small but powerful group of metalsmiths working in Suhl, and probably had its origins in the early nineteenth century. Metal goods, including a few firearms and edged weapons, were made prior to the 1890s, when large-scale bicycle production commenced — indeed, the company subsequently became known as 'C.G. Haenel Waffen- & Fahrradfabrik' (weapons and bicycle factory). M 1879 and M 1883 revolvers were made in collusion with, firstly, Schilling and Spangenberg & Sauer, and then Schilling alone. Haenel traded independently until the end of the Second World War and has now become part of the nationalised East German firearms industry.

S, Da

Spangenberg & Sauer, Suhl. This combine seems to have been the predecessor of J.P. Sauer & Sohn, and traded between about 1860 (when needle rifles were being developed) and the mid 1880s. M 1879 revolvers were made with Schilling and Haenel, but it is believed that Spangenberg died in about 1886 and the combine split up. Operations were subsequently continued by Sauer alone.

S

S

J.P. Sauer & Sohn, Suhl. This firm claimed to have been founded in 1751, but this seems more likely to have been the date on which the Sauer family first became involved in firearms manufacture; trading as a separate entity does not seem to have commenced until about 1886, when 'J. P. Sauer & Sohn' succeeded Spangenberg & Sauer. Revolvers were made in the 1880s and 1890s, initially in collaboration with Schilling and Haenel and then alone. Sauer worked in Suhl until the end of the Second World War and another company bearing the same name was founded in Eckenförde (Holstein) in 1951. This, however, has done little more than perpetuate the old trading style.

S

ERFURT
1893

Erfurt Gewehrfabrik, Erfurt, Thuringia. This Prussian government arsenal, which had been founded in Saarn bei Düsseldorf in 1815 and acquired by the government in 1851, was installed in Erfurt in 1862 and seems to have made revolvers only after about 1890. The factory was dismantled after the end of the First World War, its contents being distributed to the Allied nations as war reparations or simply sold to private contractors. The P 08 production machinery, for example, was acquired by Simson & Companie.

TABLE TWO 2

S   Da   Dr

Notes

1 '. . . Bavaria, in return for her quick response to Bismarck's call, was offered special privileges in the new Federation which would give her the illusion of independence. She was to preserve her own railway and postal systems, a limited diplomatic status in her dealings with foreign countries, and a degree of military, legal and financial autonomy. . . .': Wilfrid Blunt, *The Dream King. Ludwig II of Bavaria*, p.129.

2. The rifle was initially adopted in December 1871, but changes to the extractor delayed final acceptance for three months.

3. A copy of the Smith & Wesson 'Number 2', a sheath-trigger break-action design dating from the early 1860s.

4. Loewe made 75,000 copies of the Smith & Wesson 'Russian Model' for the Russian government in the period 1876-7/8, apparently during the period in which the parent company was supplying the genuine items.

5. Ian V. Hogg, *German Pistols and Revolvers, 1871-1945*, p.20.

6. Although no attention was initially paid to patent rights, an agreement concluded with Österreichische Waffenfabrik, to make Gewehre 88, caused a suitable royalty arrangement to be negotiated with Mannlicher and others.

7. The M 1883 was issued to mobile batteries on 12th March, 1891.

8. The encased-head safety feature was found on other nineteenth century revolvers, including the Italian No. 89. The modern Iver Johnson Supershot Sealed Eight series is just one of the designs that has since claimed 'counterbored' or 'embedded head' chambers as a novelty.

9. Hold-open devices are often used in semi-automatic pistols to hold the mechanism open after the last round has been chambered, fired and ejected. Many pistols simply utilise the magazine follower.

10. William H.J. Chamberlain, 'Faithful Soldiers of the German Empire. . .the Modell 1879 u. 1883 Deutsche Armeerevolvers', in *Gun Collector's Digest* (1975), pp.20-32.

11. Spangenberg & Sauer made needle rifles in the mid nineteenth century, though Sauer has always claimed a foundation date in 1751. This however, was not the date on which 'J.P. Sauer & Sohn' started trading.

12. The Bavarian authorities were always tardy in adopting standard weapons, usually by a few months but occasionally by a few years. Indeed, one source dating from 1894 (*Les Armes à Feu Portatives des Armes Actuelles et Leurs Munitions, par Un Officier Supérieur*) suggests that the Bavarians were still using the old single-shot Werder pistols in the *mid* 1890s.

13. The implementation regulations, or Ausführungsbestimmungen, were approved on 22nd June 1892, and proofs were applied for the first time in 1st April 1893 in houses in Oberndorf am Neckar, Suhl, Zella St Blasii and Frankfurt an der Oder.

14. See Taylerson, Andrews and Frith, *The Revolver, 1818-65*, pp. 272-82.

15. This gun is in the collection of the Armouries of the Tower of London, and is pictured in Taylerson, *The Revolver, 1865-1888*, p.133.

Data, M79 and M83—page 7.

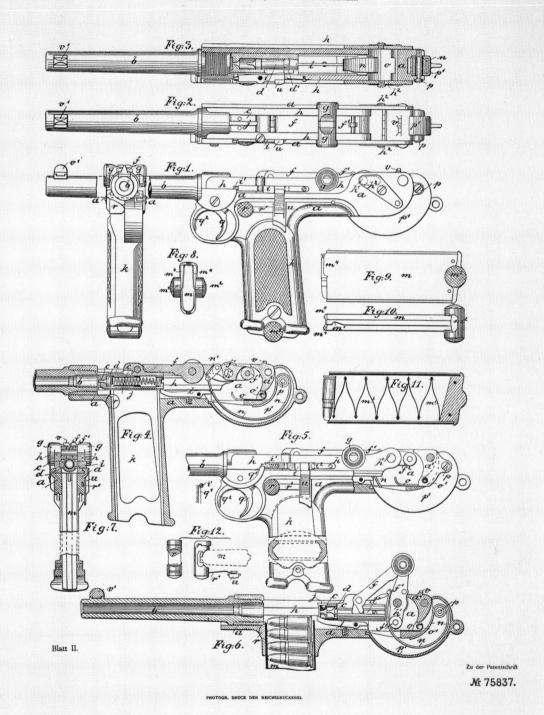

Blatt II.

Zu der Patentschrift

№ 75837.

PHOTOGR. DRUCK DER REICHSDRUCKEREI.

PART TWO

The Parabellums of 1904-18 "LUGERS"

The pistol adopted on 12th December 1904 by the Kriegsmarine, the German navy, was the first of its type to be purchased in quantity for the armed forces, although both the 1900 and 1902 patterns had undergone lengthy trials.

There were four sub-varieties of the Marine-Modell 04, though all of them were officially termed 'Modell 04' and not by the names that have since been added by modern collectors. Part of the original contract was delivered in 1905-6 and, subsequently, orders were placed in 1907, 1910 and during the First World War (1916?). The first naval guns were of a transitional design, as they represented an intermediate stage between the old model Parabellums of 1900-2 and the new model of 1904-6. The old model guns had dished toggle-grips and an inset anti-bounce lock, while the post-1906 pistols had plain knurled toggle-grips without the lock. The old-pattern riband mainspring was replaced by a coil.

Fewer than 1,500 of the original Marine-Modelle 04 were delivered, though the initial contract is variously stated to have been between eight thousand and ten thousand[1] . The original pistols are, consequently, the rarest of the sub-varieties. They had flat-faced knurled toggle-grips, a simplified one-piece anti-bounce lock being inset in the right grip. This device was intended to prevent the breechblock rebounding from the breech face as it ran forward on the loading stroke, but experience showed that it was unnecessary and it was discarded in 1904. The early Marine-Modelle had old pattern riband mainsprings, long frames, six-groove rifling, 15cm barrels and a unique two-position sliding back sight mounted on top of the rear toggle link. This was graduated for 100m and 200m, and the prominent protective sight 'wings' were most distinctive. The manual safety levers moved upwards, locking the grip safety mechanism and preventing movement of the lateral sear. After the introduction of the Pistolen 08 in 1909, and the delivery of new naval pistols in 1910-11, survivors of the earlier batches of Marine-Modelle 04 were altered so that their safety levers moved downwards.

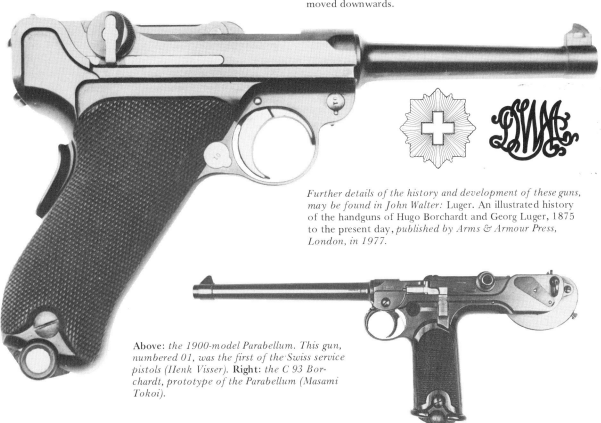

Further details of the history and development of these guns, may be found in John Walter: Luger. An illustrated history of the handguns of Hugo Borchardt and Georg Luger, 1875 to the present day, *published by Arms & Armour Press, London, in 1977.*

Above: *the 1900-model Parabellum. This gun, numbered 01, was the first of the Swiss service pistols (IIenk Visser).* **Right:** *the C 93 Borchardt, prototype of the Parabellum (Masami Tokoi).*

Improvements made to the basic Parabellum design between 1904 and 1906—the origins of which are currently in doubt[2]—caused the naval contract to be cancelled before it had been fulfilled. More guns were however, ordered in 1907, incorporating the new pattern (neuer Art, or nA) modifications: the anti-bounce lock had been discarded and a coil spring had replaced the riband pattern. The first guns, delivered between 1907 and 1909, had 'upward safe' manual lever safeties; but subsequent acquisitions had the newer 'downward safe' type, which brought the design of the naval Parabellum into line with that of the army Pistolen 08. At the same time, survivors from the earlier batches were recalled and modified so that all safety levers worked in the same direction. Only the few guns that had already been discarded owing to damage, and a few on far colonial stations, escaped.

Because so many naval Parabellums have had their safety levers altered, it is difficult to determine how many were *newly-made* with the revised safety arrangements. However, it is believed that at least 18,000 were made with the old upward-safe levers and, therefore, that only a few thousand were made with the newer pattern.

Below: *a naval Parabellum, the Pistole 04, in its last (or '1915') sub-variety — identical with the 1908 army pattern apart from the barrel length and rear sight. The case is privately made and, therefore, completely unofficial (Horst Rutsch).*

About 30,000 more Marine-Modelle were delivered to the navy between 1910-11 and the beginning of the First World War, differing solely in their safety arrangements; Georg Luger had redesigned the lever safety mechanism in 1907-8 to work directly on the lateral sear instead of on the grip safety unit. The modified design — which apparently arose from army demands for a more positive and stronger safety device — was incorporated in short-frame army Pistolen 08 and post-1910 long-frame naval guns. Marine-Modelle 04 of this sub-variety continued the use of butt-heel lugs for a board-type shoulder stock.

More naval pistols were purchased from Deutsche Waffen- und Munitionsfabriken during the First World War; a few were apparently delivered in 1916, and the bulk followed a year later. These were standard army type short-frame guns and incorporated the mechanical hold-open omitted from the 1910-14 deliveries.

All Marine-Modelle 04, despite statements made to the contrary, were made in the Berlin-Charlottenburg factory[3] of Deutsche Waffen- und Munitionsfabriken and bore the company monogram on top of the front toggle link. The first guns — the original fifteen hundred and the first 18,000 or so of the second order — had the word 'GESICHERT' lower part of the safety lever recess, exposed when the lever was moved upwards to the safe position. Those that were subsequently modified had the word erased, to be replaced by 'Gesichert' in the upper part of the recess. All later guns had an upper 'GESICHERT' mark.

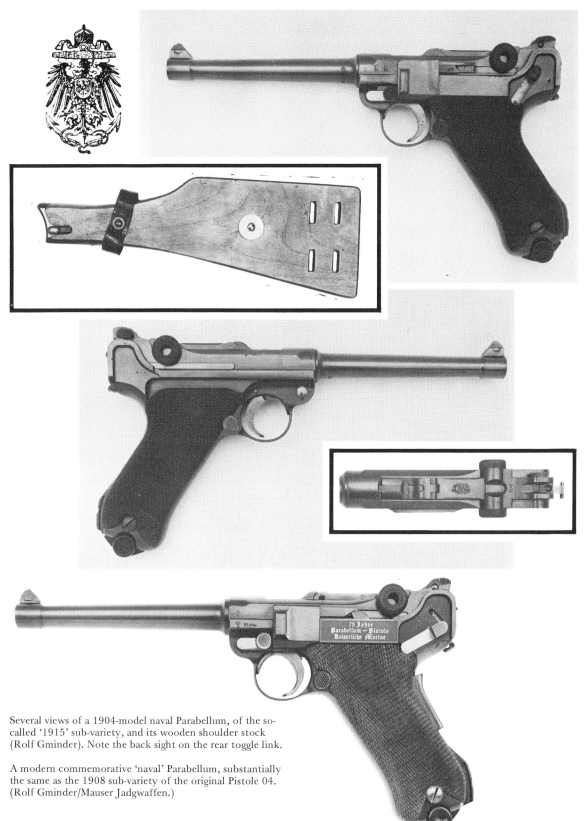

Several views of a 1904-model naval Parabellum, of the so-called '1915' sub-variety, and its wooden shoulder stock (Rolf Gminder). Note the back sight on the rear toggle link.

A modern commemorative 'naval' Parabellum, substantially the same as the 1908 sub-variety of the original Pistole 04. (Rolf Gminder/Mauser Jadgwaffen.)

Inspectors' or property marks (?), in the form of an imperial crown over 'M', were to be found struck into the underside of the barrel and twice on the left side of the receiver, while proof marks (the crown alone) appeared on the left side of the barrel, the receiver and the breechblock. Unit markings often distinguished the grip straps.

The commercial-style serial numbers appeared in full across the front of the frame and on the underside of the barrel, while the last two digits were repeated on some of the parts. The pistols made during the First World War invariably had dates above the chamber, on the left frame rail in front of the cover-plate, and on the left side of the front sight base.

It is not widely known that the German airmen (Flieger-truppen) were armed with navy Parabellums shortly before the outbreak of the First World War. Surviving correspondence between the General Inspector's branch of the military communications system (General-Inspektion des Militär-Verkehrwesens) and the weapons and equipment department of the navy office, the Reichsmarineamt, dating from March 1913, relates how one hundred 'Pistolen 04 mit Anschlagkolben' — 100 navy Parabellums with shoulder stocks — were supplied from Kiel dockyard to airfields at Döberitz, Metz, Strassburg in Elsass, Darmstadt and Köln 'shortly after' 26th March 1913, to be used pending the development of a long-barrelled derivative of the army's Pistole 08. Some navy Parabellums, together with langen Pistolen 08, are believed to have been used by pilots and observers in the opening stages of aerial combat during the First World War. However, they were quickly superseded by airborne machine-guns.

The army pistols

The success of the 1904 naval Parabellum, and the improvements made to the commercial guns marketed after 1906-7, increased the army's interest in the basic design. A slightly modified 'neuer Art' 9mm Parabellum was subsequently adopted on 22nd August 1908 as the *9mm Pistole, Modell 1908* — or 'Pistole 08', in its abbreviated form. The first issues were made on the approval of the holster, the Pistolentasche 08, on 7th April 1909.

The coil mainspring and the 1904-patented loaded-chamber indicator/extractor were retained, but the grip safety and the old manual safety were replaced by a new lever. This acted directly on the sear bar, which lay along the exposed left side of the receiver behind the cover-plate. Pistolen 08 made prior to March or April 1913 lacked stock lugs[4], but later guns had T-lugs on their butt heels. Most guns made before 1914 also lacked a mechanical hold-open. The hold-open was reinstated either shortly before the outbreak of the First World War or perhaps later in 1914, after the beginning of the field campaign. By 1914, issues of the Pistole 08 had been made to many units. (Further details may be found in the section devoted to unit markings.)

The army high command, the Oberste Heeres-Leitung (OHL), soon discovered that the Berlin-Charlottenburg DWM factory was unable to deliver enough Parabellums to satisfy the requirements of the army and navy. A duplicate set of production machinery was consequently installed in the government arsenal at Erfurt, the first guns from this source being delivered early in 1911. It has not been ascertained whether a royalty was paid to DWM and Luger on each gun made under government control, though it seems likely, as Luger was later paid a government royalty on each gun fitted with the post-1916 sear. By August 1914, DWM had delivered between 250,000 and 275,000 guns; and Erfurt, somewhere between 70,000 and 100,000.

1902-3

Parabellum development

Note particularly the revisions to the toggle-grips and the sear/safety bar area. In addition, the first guns had a grip safety device.

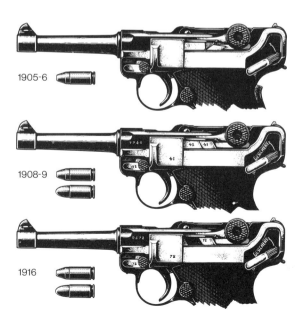

1905-6

1908-9

1916

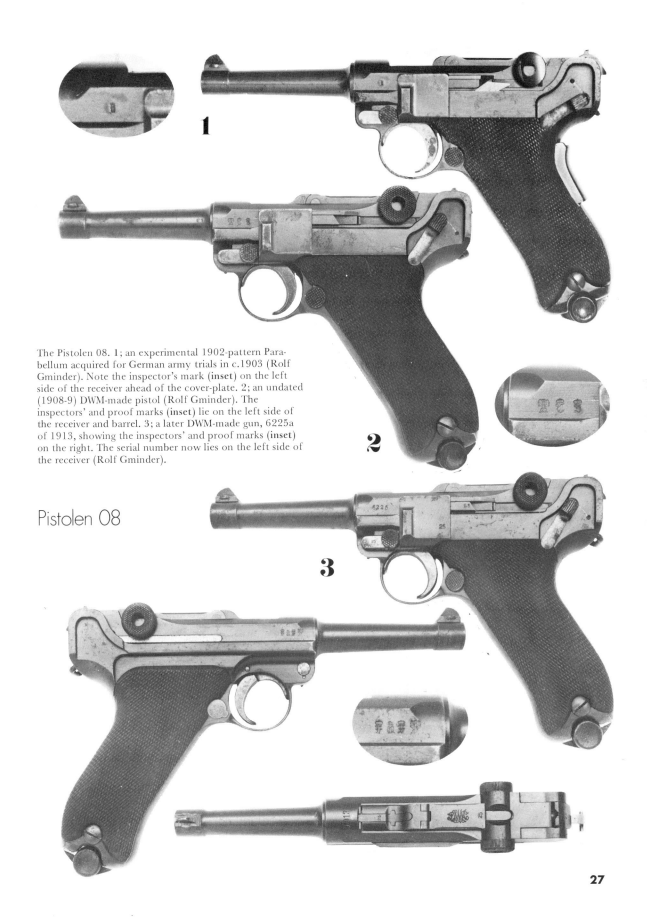

The Pistolen 08. 1; an experimental 1902-pattern Parabellum acquired for German army trials in c.1903 (Rolf Gminder). Note the inspector's mark (inset) on the left side of the receiver ahead of the cover-plate. 2; an undated (1908-9) DWM-made pistol (Rolf Gminder). The inspectors' and proof marks (inset) lie on the left side of the receiver and barrel. 3; a later DWM-made gun, 6225a of 1913, showing the inspectors' and proof marks (inset) on the right. The serial number now lies on the left side of the receiver (Rolf Gminder).

Pistolen 08

The name of the Royal Bavarian firearms factory, in Amberg, has occasionally been linked with the manufacture of Parabellums[5]. Though it is clear that none was made there, a few guns belonging to the Bavarian army could have been *repaired* there. But it is unlikely that they would have borne distinctive marks. Mystery also surrounds the small quantities of pistols said to have been made in the Spandau arsenal in 1918. There is no adequate explanation for their existence: why, for example, should the factory have tooled for the production of so complicated and expensive a pistol so near to the end of the war? From where was the production machinery obtained? And why was none found in the factory after the war?

Production of each pistol was complicated and the tools were large, numerous and expensive. Consequently only three sets of machinery are known to have existed and their movements are apparently accounted for[6]. None includes Spandau; so the questions remain. 'Correspondence' has appeared in one American gun magazine[7], purporting to show that Spandau made 7,750 or more Pistolen 08, but it must be stressed that 'evidence' of this type is purely circumstantial and can easily be faked. Similarly, many of the existing 'Spandau' pistols have been converted from Erfurt parts (which bear government inspectors' marks) and plain toggle-links.

No complete factory records, DWM or Erfurt, seem to have survived and unsubstantiated production totals of as high as two million have been published[8]. DWM seems to have made about a quarter of a million Pistolen 08 prior to August 1914 — as noted previously — and the company history, *50 Jahre Deutsche Waffen- und Munitionsfabriken*, states that a further 680,000 (approximately) P 08, LP 08 and MM 04 were made between 1st August 1914 and 11th November 1918. Erfurt's contribution is estimated to have been about 665,000 in 1911-18, which, allowing for the production of about 50,000 naval pistols by DWM prior to 1914, gives a total Parabellum production approaching 1.65 million.

It had been thought that the P 08, LP 08 and post-1914 naval pistols were numbered in separate sequences, and this had consequently led to production estimates perhaps 225,000 in excess of the total predicted by the DWM history. It now seems almost certain that *all* Parabellums made during the First World War were numbered in the same series, though the evidence is largely circumstantial. It is not possible to deduce the quantities of LP 08 and MM 04 made in 1914-18 with any degree of accuracy, though there may have been 100,000 of the former and 20,000 of the latter — and, therefore, about 1.53 million examples of the P 08, assuming all the number blocks had been completely filled.

Notes: the Spandau guns (marked *) have never been satisfactorily authenticated. Erfurt's production of Pistolen 08 should be considered as a minimum, as no gun dated '1915' has yet been discovered.

Parabellum production
Table three

 Each symbol represents 100,000 pistols

DWM MM 04, 1905–18 **70,000+**	
DWM P 08, 1909–18 **825,000**	
Erfurt P 08, 1911–18 **650,000**?	
Spandau P 08, 1918 only **200**✳	
DWM and Erfurt LP 08, 1914–18 **100,000**?	
TOTAL, all gun types, 1905–18 **1,645,200+**	

Even production on such a large scale could not satisfy the army needs and the authorities were forced to purchase less efficient weapons such as the FL-Selbstlader, the 7.65mm ACP Dreyse, the Beholla and others. The serviceable revolvers were brought out of store and a contract for 150,000 Mauser-Selbstladepistolen C 96 – chambering the standard 9mm Pistolenpatrone 08 – was placed in 1915[9].

Wartime alterations to the Parabellum included a modification to the sear bar, protected by German patent 312,919 of 1st April 1916, which allowed the mechanism to be loaded with the safety catch applied. The sear was simply cut away in front of the safety bar, which otherwise prevented its longitudinal movement. Consequently, the receiver could slide back far enough for the toggle to be completely opened, and the breechblock loaded the chamber as it was returned. But the safety bar still prevented the sear being operated to release the striker. Luger received a one Mark royalty on each new sear and the large quantity of new guns made after 1916, together with older guns altered as they came back for repair, made him a small fortune. The pistols fitted with the new-pattern sear were generally called 'mit Abzugsstange neuer Art' ('with new-pattern sear bar') while the unaltered guns were 'mit Abzugsstange alter Art'. These designations have been seen shortened to 'm Abz nA' and 'm Abz aA'.

A few pistols were transformed into rudimentary machine-pistols by modifying the sear mechanism so that the toggle tripped the sear bar, the trigger taking no part in the cycle until it was finally released. These experimental weapons were issued with the 32-round Trommelmagazine 08. However, the whole project was subsequently abandoned in favour of the Bergmann Maschinenpistole 18. One gun[10] was fitted with a 30cm Maxim-pattern silencer, but its special low-power ammunition doomed the project from the start.

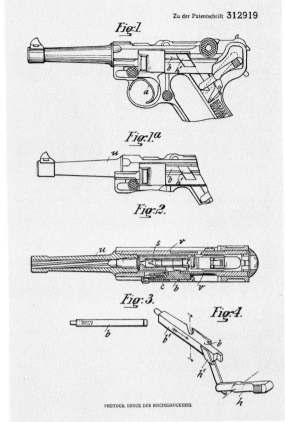

Above: *drawings of the modified sear-bar, German patent 312,919 of 1916.* Below: *the Parabellum-Navarro machine pistol, invented by two Mexicans just prior to the First World War and typical of contemporary experiments.*

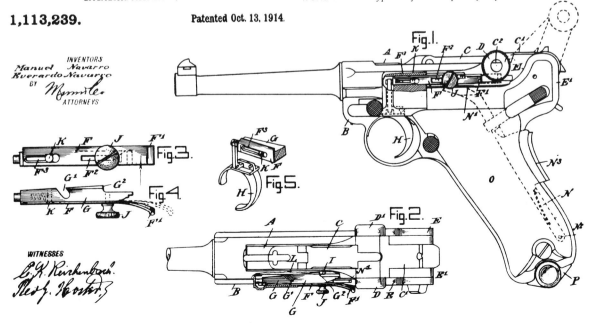

Pistole 08 **principal parts**

The barrel and receiver assembly, with the sear bar and its spring in place.

The toggle unit, breechblock and bell-crank lever. The last-named piece transmitted the power of the coil-type mainspring to the toggle mechanism.

The firing-pin, its spring and follower. This assembly is usually found inside the breechblock.

The frame with the trigger, the safety lever mechanism and the coil-pattern mainspring in position. Note the dismantling catch rotated downwards in front of the trigger guard.

The cover-plate, containing the intermediate lever that permits pressure on the trigger to release the sear.

The grips.

The magazine.

The major components of the Pistole 08 (Ian Hogg).

The lang Pistole

Much confusion surrounds the introduction of the so-called 'artillery Parabellum', which was simply a long-barrelled derivative of the Pistole 08. Various guesses — generally without substantiation — have been published; some have stated that its introduction took place in 1911, more in 1914 and others in 1917. Typical of the last is Ian Hogg's claim[11] : *In 1917 came the long-barrelled 'Artillery' model. It appears to have been issued for service in August or September 1917, the first specimens falling into Allied hands during a trench raid in the Loos sector in September. . . .*

Evidence of capture, however, is rarely a reliable guide to an introduction date and in this case is wrong; coincidentally, the British Small Arms Committee had tested the Karabiner 98 in 1916 as a 'New German Rifle' — and it had been adopted in 1909! The orders relating to the introduction of the long Parabellum were signed in mid 1913. Their text reads: *Auf den mir gehaltenen Vortrag genehmige Ich das Mir vorgelegte Muster einer Selbstladepistole mit Schulterstück unter der Benennung "Lange Pistole 08". In Ergänzung Meiner Ordre vom 22. August 1908 bestimme Ich, dass die Feldartillerie und die Flieger nach Massgabe der verfügbaren Mittel mit der langen Pistole bewaffnet werden. Ausserdem kann sie in der Ausrüstung der Festungen Aufnahme sinden. Das Kriegsministerium hat das Weitere zu veranlassen. Berlin, den 3.Juli 1913— (signed) Wilhelm*

Adoption papers for the Lang Pistole 08, 1913. 1, 2, Prussia; 3, Bavaria (Reinhard Kornmayer).

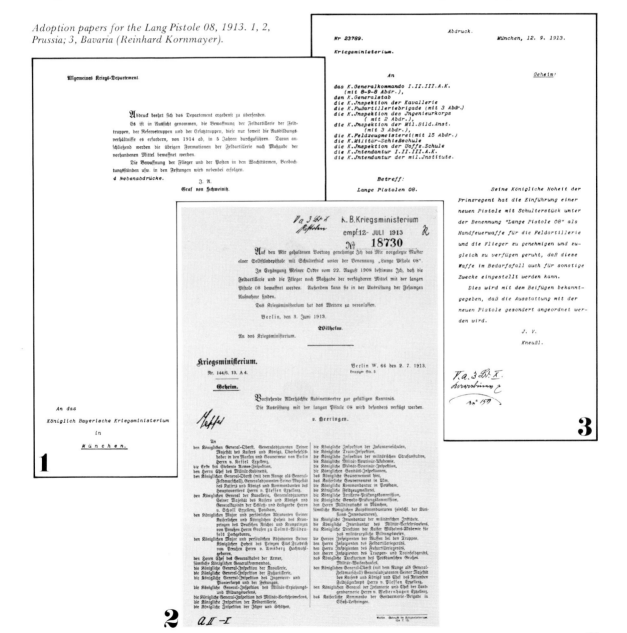

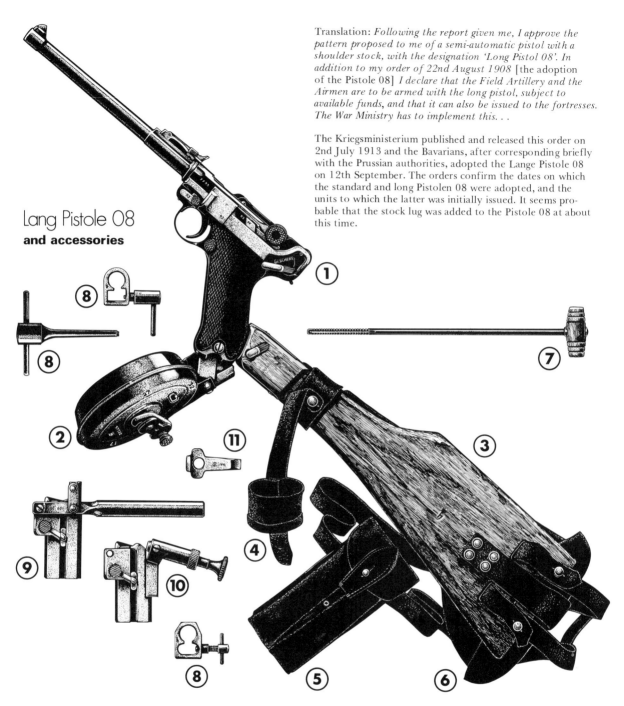

Lang Pistole 08
and accessories

Translation: *Following the report given me, I approve the pattern proposed to me of a semi-automatic pistol with a shoulder stock, with the designation 'Long Pistol 08'. In addition to my order of 22nd August 1908* [the adoption of the Pistole 08] *I declare that the Field Artillery and the Airmen are to be armed with the long pistol, subject to available funds, and that it can also be issued to the fortresses. The War Ministry has to implement this. . .*

The Kriegsministerium published and released this order on 2nd July 1913 and the Bavarians, after corresponding briefly with the Prussian authorities, adopted the Lange Pistole 08 on 12th September. The orders confirm the dates on which the standard and long Pistolen 08 were adopted, and the units to which the latter was initially issued. It seems probable that the stock lug was added to the Pistole 08 at about this time.

Key to drawings — 1, lang Pistole 08; 2, Trommelmagazin 08; 3, stock; 4, stock 'boot'; 5, two-magazine pouch; 6, holster; 7, cleaning rod; 8, sight adjusting tools; 9, magazine loader; 10, magazine unloader (one known, authenticity suspect); and 11, combined screwdriver and stripping tool.

The official manual for the Lange Pistole 08, *Anleitung zur langen Pistole 08 mit ansteckbarem Trommelmagazin (T.M.),* states that: *On account of its high firepower and easy handling, when employed as a light carbine, it* [the Lange Pistole 08] *can be used effectively against 'head size' targets at a distance of 600 metres. Accuracy to 800 metres is possible if the back sight is adjusted accordingly. When careful aim is taken, all targets will be hit at 200 metres. The bullet will penetrate horses' skulls and steel helmets at 800 metres. . .*

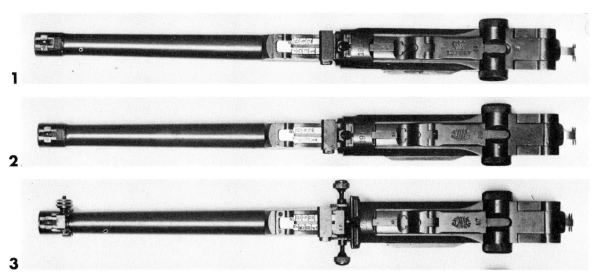

1

2

3

Three langen Pistolen 08 (Rolf Gminder): 1, made at the government-owned Erfurt factory, 1914; 2, DWM-made, 1915; 3, DWM-made in 1917, fitted with micro-adjustable sights (not contemporary with the original gun).

Lang Pistole 08: handbook

Nur für den Dienstgebrauch!

**Anleitung
zur langen Pistole 08
mit ansteckbarem
Trommelmagazin.**
(T. M.)

Berlin 1917.

Tafel V.

a. Magazinwechsel
bei nicht leergeschossenem
Magazin

Zurückziehen des Verschlusses
T. M. auf den Oberschenkel
aufgesetzt

b. Zusammensetzen der Pistole.
(Aufschieben des Griffstücks auf die Hülse)

The pistols were standard new pattern Parabellums with 20cm barrels and tangent leaf-sights mounted on the barrel in front of the receiver. Their mechanism was identical with that of the standard Pistole 08, without the anti-bounce lock and the grip safeties found on some earlier Parabellums. Luger's combined extractor and loaded-chamber indicator was fitted in the breechblock, and a 'downward safe' manual safety lever was recessed in the rear left side of the frame. The sights were generally constructed with a 'bias', in which elevation automatically compensated for bullet drift at long ranges. The sight leaves were invariably graduated from 0 to 800 metres in 100m steps. The front and back sights of some guns could be laterally adjusted by set-screws and capstan tools. All Langen Pistolen 08 had short frames, and most were made in the DWM Berlin-Charlottenburg or Berlin-Wittenau factories[12]. A few, however, are known to have been made at Erfurt — though production in the government arsenal was far exceeded by production in the private DWM factories. After 1916, there were pistols with the old pattern sear bar ('Langen Pistolen 08 mit Abzugsstangen alter Art') and with the new type ('Langen Pistolen 08 mit Abzugsstangen neuer Art'). The official handbook, dated 1917, clearly recognises the distinction.

The official army handbook says of the drum magazine:

A. Purpose
1. The Trommelmagazin increases the firepower of the Pistole 08 considerably, since its capacity is 32 rounds rather than 8.
2. The Trommelmagazin can be used with either short or long Pistolen 08. The higher performance of the Lange Pistole 08 — owing to its longer barrel, the fact that its sights are graduated to 800m and the shoulder stock provision — make it a formidable weapon for close combat, repulsing assaults and special duties, especially when fitted with the Trommelmagazin.

C. Instructions
1. General
The dust cover should only be removed when loading, unloading, or when the magazine is inserted in the pistol. The Trommelmagazin can only be loaded when removed from the pistol, and only with the loading tool provided. The magazines should never be left loaded, as this can strain the driving and follower springs. Even when the magazine is empty the tensioning device must be released in order to protect the driving spring.

The lang Pistole 08 fitted with its drum magazine, the Trommelmagazin 08 (Masami Tokoi), and the magazine itself (Rolf Gminder). There were several minor variants of the magazine.

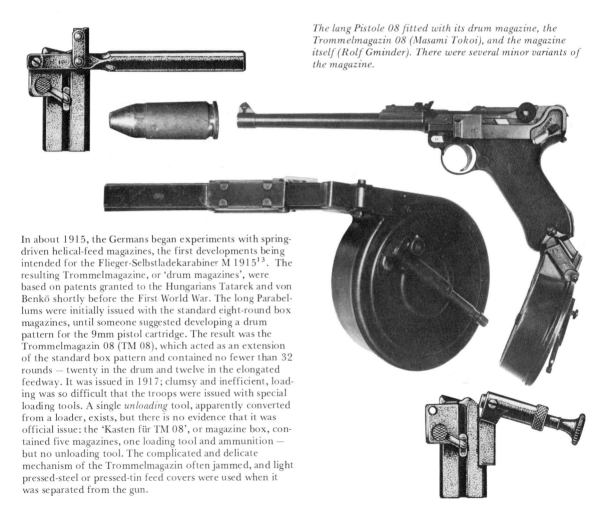

In about 1915, the Germans began experiments with spring-driven helical-feed magazines, the first developments being intended for the Flieger-Selbstladekarabiner M 1915[13]. The resulting Trommelmagazine, or 'drum magazines', were based on patents granted to the Hungarians Tatarek and von Benkö shortly before the First World War. The long Parabellums were initially issued with the standard eight-round box magazines, until someone suggested developing a drum pattern for the 9mm pistol cartridge. The result was the Trommelmagazin 08 (TM 08), which acted as an extension of the standard box pattern and contained no fewer than 32 rounds — twenty in the drum and twelve in the elongated feedway. It was issued in 1917; clumsy and inefficient, loading was so difficult that the troops were issued with special loading tools. A single *unloading* tool, apparently converted from a loader, exists, but there is no evidence that it was official issue: the 'Kasten für TM 08', or magazine box, contained five magazines, one loading tool and ammunition — but no unloading tool. The complicated and delicate mechanism of the Trommelmagazin often jammed, and light pressed-steel or pressed-tin feed covers were used when it was separated from the gun.

Long Parabellums were usually issued with board-type shoulder stocks, which fitted to the stock lug on the butt heel. A leather holster, and spare box-magazine pouches were often attached to the stock body. It has been reported that many of these pistols were withdrawn from the artillery towards the end of the First World War and reissued to sailors manning the navy's gunboats and inshore minesweepers. Very few had been examined with anything other than army unit marks, however, and the reports remained largely unsubstantiated until information about an artillery shoulder-stock with naval markings was received from a collector in the USA, Thompson D. Knox. It has no army inspectors' marks — which are inevitably present on standard army-issue items — and its marking disc, possibly added after manufacture, bears the marks of Torpedo-Division Nr. 2 ('II.T.D.333.'). Naval 'crown M' property or inspectors' markings are struck into both sides of the stock body.

The original number of the stock was 3881c, which, if there was the slightest doubt, shows it to be an artillery pattern: no naval 1904-model Parabellum is known to have borne a 'c' suffix number. The stock does not fit the naval pistols, since naval and artillery specimens were not usually interchangeable. The position of the locking catch is sufficiently different to prevent stocks locking properly on 'wrong' gun models.

Markings

Maker's marks. There are only two of these: the distinctive DWM monogram and the crown/ERFURT mark applied by the Prussian government's arsenal at Erfurt, in Thüringen. The authenticity of the crown/SPANDAU (and, for that matter, crown/AMBERG) mark remains questionable.

Serial numbers. See Table 5 for the distribution of the numbers and part-numbers.

Date of manufacture. This did not appear on pistols made by Deutsche Waffen- & Munitionsfabriken prior to 1910, but may be found on the receivers of all guns made thereafter by DWM (1910-18), Erfurt (1911-18) and, purportedly, Spandau (1918 only).

Proof marks. Considerable controversy exists over the distinction between proof and inspectors' marks. The only genuine proof marks are the displayed eagles found on the right side of the receiver (left, on pre-1910 DWM guns), the barrel, the breechblock, and occasionally on the frame and the rear toggle cross-pin (generally confined to Erfurt products). The DWM and Erfurt proof eagles, or Beschussadler, were of markedly different design — as shown.

Inspectors' and assemblers' marks. These also present several mysteries, since the distinction between them and the proof marks is easily blurred and, consequently, misunderstood. The inspectors' marks take the form of small crowned gothic-letter punches, some of which are especially notable alongside the proof eagles struck into the receiver. Each gun underwent inspection and proof several times during the final stages of assembly and finish, each step being marked by the stamping of an inspector's letter. Costanzo, in *World of Lugers: Proof Marks,* states that *receiver proofs used on DWM/Erfurt Lugers have all been said to be inspectors' proofs. This author feels that these are not; I believe the proofs to be contract codes, destination points and lot numbers. . . ,* but he is most probably wrong — as all German rifles, for example, have similar sets of inspectors' marks on their barrels and receivers. These components were provably submitted to several tests and inspections before being passed as fit for service.

Table four
Inspectors' letter-marks
Parabellums

These stamped letters, which may be found alongside the displayed eagle proof mark on the right side of the receiver (on the left on early DWM-made Pistolen 08), have been catalogued from a number of sources — often for what they *appear* to be, rather than what they actually are. It is often difficult for a non-German to distinguish between, for instance, the fraktur 'Z' and 'B' and it is likely that some of the letter combinations below have been misread: 'DCN' could easily be 'DGN', and 'BMP' may be the same as 'BMB'. This should be borne in mind when assessing a mark on an undated gun or one from which the date has been removed.

There may well have been other letter combinations, as research has not been completed; the author will be grateful for any further information.

Note: Pistolen 08 made by Deutsche Waffen- & Munitionsfabriken in 1908-9 were not dated above their chambers. Letter combinations found on these weapons are marked in the table with an asterisk (*).

BBP	Erfurt 1918	CC	Erfurt 1911	DCN	Erfurt 1912 (?)	EE	DWM 1908-9*, 1911; Erfurt 1911 (?)	FFP	Erfurt 1916-17
BCP	Erfurt 1917	CF	Erfurt 1912	DCO	Erfurt 1912			FMP	Erfurt 1917
BDR	Erfurt 1918	CGO	Erfurt 1912	DCS	Erfurt 1913			FPS	Erfurt 1912
BFB	Erfurt 1918	CGR	Erfurt 1911	DFP	Erfurt 1916	EEX	DWM 1914	FQF	DWM 1913
BFP	Erfurt 1912, 1917-18	CHB	Erfurt 1912	DGC	Erfurt 1913	EG	DWM 1908-9*	FQP	Erfurt 1916
		CHR	Erfurt 1912	DGN	Erfurt 1912	EO	DWM 1911-12	FRP	Erfurt 1917
BMB	Erfurt 1918	CL	Erfurt 1912 (?)	DID	Erfurt 1913	EUBD	Spandau 1918 (?)	FUR	DWM 1916; Erfurt 1916
BMP	Erfurt 1917-18	COE	Erfurt 1913	DSE	Erfurt 1913				
BOE	Erfurt 1913	CQ	DWM 1908-9*	DU	DWM 1908-9*			FWT	Erfurt 1916
BRB	Erfurt 1918	CR	Erfurt 1911	DUD	Erfurt 1913				
BSE	Erfurt 1913	CSS	DWM 1918	DUN	Erfurt 1912				
BSS	Erfurt 1916	CZ	DWM 1908-9*						
BUD	Erfurt 1912								
BUS	Erfurt 1913								
BXP	Erfurt 1918								
HHF	DWM 1913	ICP	Erfurt 1917	LLD	DWM 1912	MLB	Erfurt 1914	OFP	Erfurt 1913-14
HPP	DWM 1916	IF	Erfurt 1917	LLF	DWM 1912				
HRR	DWM 1916	IGP	Erfurt 1917	LLL	DWM 1913				
HSS	DWM 1915-18	IHP	Erfurt 1917	LLV	DWM 1913 (?)				
		IOP	Erfurt 1917						
		IRP	Erfurt 1917						
RMB	Erfurt 1918	SES	DWM 1914-15	T	DWM 1917-18	U	Erfurt 1914	WLB	DWM 1916
RPS	Spandau 1918	SEX	DWM 1914	TD	DWM 1911	UHB	Erfurt 1914	WPB	Erfurt 1914 (?); DWM 1916
		SSS	DWM 1915	TI	DWM 1912 (?)	ULB	Erfurt 1914		
				TO	DWM 1911	UMP	Erfurt 1914	WVP	DWM 1916
				TS	DWM 1917-18	UOB	Erfurt 1914		
				TSS	DWM 1917-18	UOF	Erfurt 1914		
				TT	DWM 1908-9*, 1910	USB	Erfurt 1914		
				TZ	DWM 1908-9*, 1910-11	USD	Erfurt 1914		
						UUE	Erfurt 1914		
XQE	DWM 1913	ZX	DWM, 1914?						
XQF	DWM 1913-14								
XQM	DWM 1913								
XQT	DWM 1914								
XX	DWM 1913-14								

TABLE FOUR 2

The government arsenal at Erfurt seems to have used more inspectors than the privately-run DWM plant, even though the latter's were nonetheless military personnel. However, the DWM inspectors seem to have been changed less often (compare, particularly, 1917 and 1918).

It has been suggested that each punch represented the initial letter of the inspectors' surname, but this lacks substantiation – particularly as the letter 'X' appears regularly (it may have been used as a substitute for punches that would otherwise have been difficult to decipher). However, the letters found alongside the receiver proof mark do undoubtedly fall into several clearly defined groupings.

Erfurt pistols usually had a single inspector's mark on each part – the dismantling lever, the cover plate, the grip screws, etc. – while DWM-made guns did not. Both have assemblers' marks in the frame well, on the underside of the receiver stop lug, and elsewhere[14].

Occasional alterations were made to the Pistolen 08 and, consequently, to the inspection procedures. Many of the earliest guns, whether made by DWM or Erfurt, were recalled in 1914-15 and fitted with hold-open devices – which had been omitted from the original design. They have an additional inspectors' mark alongside the hold-open retaining pin where it runs through the frame. Some

of the pistols made by DWM prior to 1910 (with their receiver proof and inspectors' marks on the left rather than the right, and undated chambers) were given additional receiver-side serial numbers and auxiliary parts-numbers at some time in their pre-1918 service careers; these marks are *not* original.

Miscellaneous marks. There is inevitably a calibre mark such as '8,82' (8.82mm bore diameter) on the underside of the barrel immediately ahead of the frame. And there may be one or more unit marks on the grip strap.

Notes

1. W.L. 'Dick' Deibel, 'The "Dutch" Luger', in *Guns Review*, January 1974, page 15.

2. W.L. 'Dick' Deibel, 'The "Dutch" Luger', in *Guns Review*, January, February and March 1974, suggests that the basic changes were the work of Dutch technicians in Hembrug.

3. The production machinery was transferred from Berlin-Charlottenburg to Berlin-Wittenau at the end of 1916. Production started there in 1917. See a letter from W. Stonley, Darlington, in *Guns Review*, February 1977, p.63, quoting the company history *50 Jahre Deutsche Waffen- und Munitionsfabriken Aktiengesellschaft*.

4. The addition of these lugs is, however, often assumed to have been contemporary with the issue of the langen Pistolen 08.

5. Fred Datig, *The Luger Pistol*, p.127, note 1.

6. There were, as far as is known, only three sets of production machinery. The first, owned by DWM, was transferred from Berlin-Charlottenburg to Berlin-Wittenau in 1916-17, and subsequently to Mauser-Werke's Oberndorf factory in 1930. The second was installed in the Erfurt arsenal in 1910, acquired by Simson & Co. after the First World War and sold to Krieghoff in 1935. The third was installed in the Eidgenössische Waffenfabrik, Bern, in 1918 and remained there until the 1950s.

7. Helms and Evans, 'Lugers, Holsters and Accessories. A collector's guide to values', in *Guns of the World* (1972), pp. 310-23.

8. Datig, *The Luger Pistol*, p. 123 — and others, mostly basing their claims on Datig's.

9. The contract was never completed, as only about 140,000 guns were delived before the Armistice.

10. Datig, *The Luger Pistol*, pp. 145-7.

11. Ian Hogg, *German Pistols and Revolvers, 1871-1945*, p.75.

12. Production in Berlin-Wittenau began in 1917.

13. The Mexican-designed Mondragon semi-automatic rifle, small quantities of which were acquired from SIG during the First World War, was used experimentally in aerial and trench warfare; the trials were uninspiring, however, and the guns were subsequently withdrawn.

14. Harry E. Jones, *Luger Variations (Volume One)*, pp. 238-9.

Data, Pistole 08–page 7.

Gun:		DWM	P08, 1909	P08, 1915	
Marks found on:	Barrel, left side		⚜	—	✳
	Barrel, right side		—	⚜	✳
	Barrel, underside		9113 8,82	5771b 8,83	✳
	Frame front, outer surface		9113	5771 b	✳
	Breechblock, left side		13 and ⚜	71 and ⚜	✳
	Extractor, underside		13	—	
	Extractor, top		—	71	
	Extractor, left side		GELADEN	GELADEN	✳
	Front toggle, link, top		DWM	71 and DWM	✳
	Front toggle link, underside		13	—	
	Rear toggle link, back		13	71	
	Manual safety lever, top edge		—	71	
	Sear blocking blade, outer surface		—	71	
	Sear bar, outer surface		—	71	
	Frame recess, left rear		GESICHERT	GESICHERT	✳
	Receiver, chamber top		—	1915	✳
	Receiver, left side		⚜ ▦	5771	✳
	Receiver, right side		—	▦ ⚜	✳
	Receiver, bottom of stop lug		13		
	Sear bar, underside		13*	—	
	Trigger, left side		13	71	
	Cover plate, bottom		13	—	
	Cover plate, outer surface		—	71	
	Dismantling catch, end		13*	—	
	Dismantling catch, outer surface		—	71	
	Magazine crossbolt, right side		13*	71	
	Hold-open, top surface		not fitted	71	
✱ Not always present	Grips, inner surface		9113	5771	
✳ Important marking	Magazine bottom piece		9113	5771b	✳

Table five   **Typical pistol markings**

The Mauser-Pistole C96

The C 96 was the only other locked-breech design bought during the First World War. The Oberste Heeres Leitung found that the output of Deutsche Waffen- und Munitions-fabriken and the government arsenal in Erfurt was far from sufficient to satisfy the demands for pistols, and contracts were placed with commercial manufacturers such as Walther and Langenhan early in 1915. These led to the issue of thousands of blowback weapons such as the Walther Modell 4 and the FL-Selbstlader. As Deiss[1] noted, . . . *The Pistole 08 was used by non-commissioned officers without rifles, machine gunners, hospital personnel and infantry stretcher-bearers, and by cavalry non-commissioned officers without lances. The gunners of the field artillery — in addition to the non-commissioned officers and drivers — carried the M 79 or M 83 revolver on field service. They were re-armed with the Pistole 08 or the Mauser pistol [C96] with holster stock during the course of the war. The latter was issued, as far as possible, to the machine-gun companies. The shortage of pistols forced the issue of more than thirty different types, large and small, to the machine-gunners and personnel of the army medical corps . . . Officers' armament, however, had shown such variety since the beginning of the war.*

Sometime in late 1915 — the precise date is not yet known — the authorities approached Waffenfabrik Mauser, intending to purchase an unknown number of C 96 pistols. It has always been assumed that the order was for 150,000 though no satisfactory documentary evidence in support of this claim has been produced. The C 96 has been developed by the three Feederle brothers, and latterly by Mauser himself in the last decade of the nineteenth century: ironically, around the original 7.65mm Borchardt cartridge. By the period of the First World War, the design of the C 96 had been stabilised, having undergone several frame-machining revisions, the addition of a second locking lug, and several changes in the safety mechanism; and an early reputation for jamming had been forgotten.

Trials held in Britain in the early 1900s had been very uncomplimentary about the Mauser. A report of the CISA[2], in July 1901, had shown 55 jams in 180 rounds, though this had been largely due to a weak magazine follower spring. Another, from the Captain of HMS *Excellent*, WO Paper 77/19/1459 of September 1901, said of the Mauser: *Advantages — Nil. Disadvantages — Perpetual jams. Bad feed. Unsafe. Pistol when loaded and cocked will fire when the safety catch is moved from "safe" to "fire" (without touching the trigger or hammer).*

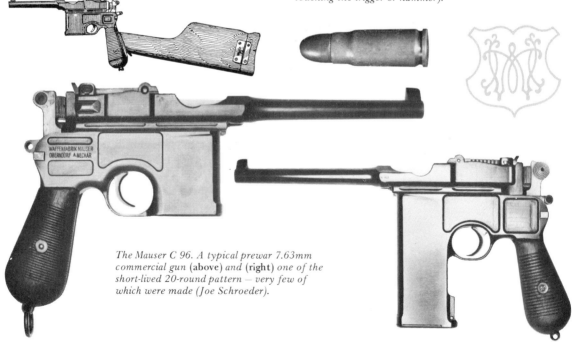

The Mauser C 96. A typical prewar 7.63mm commercial gun (above) and (right) one of the short-lived 20-round pattern — very few of which were made (Joe Schroeder).

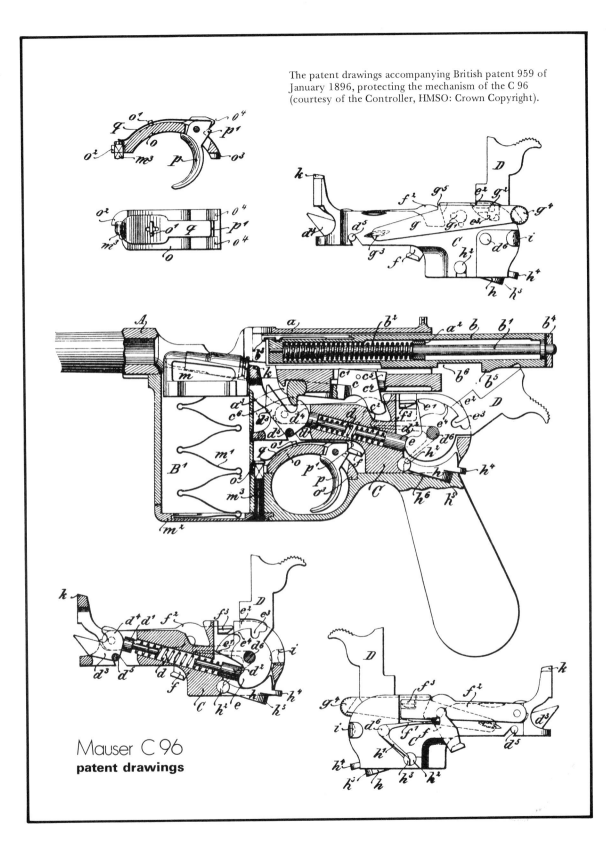

The patent drawings accompanying British patent 959 of January 1896, protecting the mechanism of the C 96 (courtesy of the Controller, HMSO: Crown Copyright).

Mauser C 96
patent drawings

Several military trials of the C 96, usually promoted by the enthusiastic Generalmajor z.D. Richard Wille[3], had been undertaken between 1896 (when the Kaiser had personally tested one) and the early twentieth century. But the Parabellum had been quite properly preferred, since it was a much handier weapon with a removable box magazine, and the C 96 had been ignored in Germany even though small numbers had been issued in Turkey, Italy and Persia.

However, the Mausers acquired by the German army during the First World War were chambered for the standard 9mm Parabellum cartridge, which, because it was shorter than the standard 7.63mm and 9mm Export Mauser types, does not seem to have given feed trouble. By the 1930s — according to Mauser's literature, at least — the feed problems with the standard 7.63mm cartridge had been completely eliminated as well. The handbook for the 'Modell 1930' states that *One pistol fired an uninterrupted series of 2,200 rounds, rapid fire, without the least injury, or any intervening cleaning or attention other than cooling the barrel after every 300 rounds. Another fired 11,000 rounds without a single malfunction, loss of accuracy, or measurable wear . . .*

The recoil-operated C 96, locked by a propped-up block beneath the bolt, was an extremely clumsy pistol; and its charger-loaded fixed magazine was inferior to the detachable Parabellum pattern. However, despite its faults, the Mauser seems to have been greatly valued by the men to whom it was issued, as it was accurate and powerful. Like the long-barrelled version of the Pistole 08, the C 96 made an acceptable light carbine when fitted with its detachable holster stock.

The contract placed with Mauser does not seem to have been completed, as only about 140,000 guns were delivered to the army prior to the armistice, and, therefore, the quantity fell about ten thousand short of what is usually assumed to have been the negotiated figure. The observed serial numbers range from 4 to 137033, and Belford & Dunlap[4] suggest that the series' prototype was a converted '9mm Export' C 96, number 179064.

The genuine 9mm Parabellum Mausers can usually be recognised by the figure '9' cut into the horizontally ribbed wooden grips and generally stained red (although some black ones, which may be no more than aged red, have also been recorded). A few pistols have been reported with plain grips, the insides of which are serialled to the guns as the '9' patterns had been. The quality of the finish and machining was noticeably inferior to that of the standard commercial variations, many of which also found their way into military service. The grips of the 9mm Parabellum guns — for example — often fit very poorly, though the weapons are structurally sound. Their tangent-leaf backsights were graduated from 50 to 500 metres in 50m increments.

The military guns bear serial numbers on the receiver, or barrel extension, alongside the chamber area, and also on the rear grip strap and inside the grips. A standard commercial proof mark (crown, crown U) appears on the left side of the chamber and a government inspector's mark, usually a crown over the gothic letter M, can be found on the right. The maker's mark, WAFFENFABRIK MAUSER over OBERNDORF A/N, appears in three lines above the chamber and WAFFENFABRIK MAUSER OBERNDORF A/NECKAR in two lines on the rear right side of the frame,

between the two milled-out panels. Many guns also bear a stylised displayed or spread eagle — probably a property or acceptance mark in view of its position — on the front outer surface of the magazine well.

The pistols were issued in wooden holster stocks of the type pictured, resting in leather harnesses. Unit markings are occasionally found on the lid of the holster stock and on the front grip strap of the pistols. They may even prove to be naval markings, since some guns were re-issued to the Kriegsmarine towards the end of the First World War and are occasionally reported with the distinctive naval 'crown over M'.

Notes

1. Major a.D. F.W. Deiss, *Ehrenbuch des Deutschen Heeres*, volume 2.

2. The Chief Inspector of Small Arms. It was also recorded that only four malfunctions occurred in 180 rounds when the gun was fired with the holster stock attached. It was felt that this reduced the upward 'kick' and prevented the weight of the cartridge column forcing downwards on the follower spring in such a way that it could not properly reassert itself.

3. The author of several books and pamphlets praising the C 96. It is believed that he was a Mauser consultant, and, consequently, that his comments were not always unbiased.

4. James Belford and Jack Dunlap: *The Mauser Self-Loading Pistol*, page 128.

PART FOUR

Holsters and accessories

The holster issued with the M 1879 commission revolver, introduced on 31st August 1881, was known as the 'Revolvertasche M 81' (M 82 in Bavaria). It had a long slender leather body and a large protective 'bucket' flap covering all but the tip of the revolver butt. A strap on the flap engaged a tongued buckle stitched to the body. Unit and maker's markings will often be found inside the flap or on the back of the holster body.

The backs of M 81 holsters intended for dismounted troops each had two belt loops, as the guns were worn on the left hip with the butts angled forwards. Examples issued to mounted personnel had the loops continued upwards above the line of the flap, attached to a leather plate. These were worn on the right hip. Cartridges were carried in the Kartusche M 81, on a separate bandolier, while the cleaning rod — which doubled as an ejector — could be found on the top of the cartridge-box flap. A leather lanyard ran from the revolver's butt-ring to the bandolier, preventing the pistol being lost.

The smaller holster for the M 83 revolver, introduced on 12th March 1891 and consequently designated 'M 91' (M 92 in Bavaria), did not have a conventional flap. Instead, a long leather strap extended backwards over the sheathed revolver until it could be slipped over a stud on the holster body, behind and below the trigger guard. This prevented the hammer snagging on clothing and also protected the gun. A small cartridge pouch, closed by a conventional strap-and-buckle device, was stitched onto the front of the M 91 holster body.

Holsters for the 1904-type naval Parabellum existed in at least three varieties. The earliest, made of black leather, had a plain pointed flap — lacking the 'bucket' or rainproof edges of the later Pistolentasche 08 — and a simple slot-and-stud closure, rather than the more sophisticated strap and buckle. A pocket for the cleaning rod appeared on the holster spine and two loops for a carrying strap were stitched to the back of the holster body. These naval holsters were always issued with a wooden shoulder-stock and a separate leather pouch containing two extra magazines.

The second version of the Pistolentasche 04 had two belt loops (appreciably larger than those for the carrying strap) and a rounded rather than pointed flap. The third variety had a standard army-style strap and buckle closure. In common with the second pattern, it was not issued with the wooden stock.

The naval shoulder stock was a flat board type, similar to its later 'artillery' counterpart issued with the langen Pistolen 08. About 2cm shorter than the artillery issue, the naval stock usually had a brass marking-disc inlet on the left side — a feature lacking on army LP 08 examples.

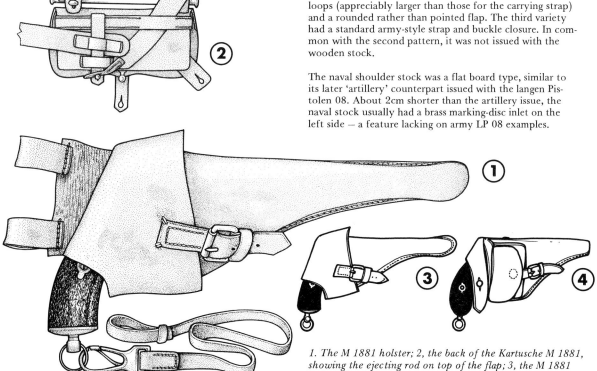

1. The M 1881 holster; 2, the back of the Kartusche M 1881, showing the ejecting rod on top of the flap; 3, the M 1881 holster for foot troops; and 4, the M 1891 holster.

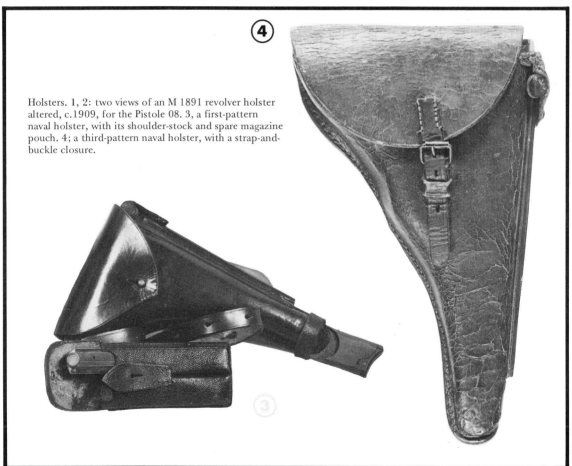

Holsters. 1, 2: two views of an M 1891 revolver holster
altered, c.1909, for the Pistole 08. 3, a first-pattern
naval holster, with its shoulder-stock and spare magazine
pouch. 4; a third-pattern naval holster, with a strap-and-
buckle closure.

The original holsters for the army's Pistole 08, probably made in 1908-9, were converted from Revolvertaschen M 91; their unusual shape, with characteristic flowing lines, is most distinctive. The original holster-front cartridge pouch was replaced by a pocket on the spine, which accepted the auxiliary pistol magazine. These holsters are very rarely found and it can only be concluded that few were made, presumably for large-scale troop trials preceding the formal introduction of the Pistole 08 on 22nd August 1908.

The perfected Pistolentasche 08 was made of brown, black or blackened-brown leather and had a distinctive shaped or 'bucket' flap designed to keep water and mud out of the holster body. A strap on the outside of the flap ran through a buckle attached to the body, and a tongue on the buckle passed through holes punched in the holster strap to prevent accidental opening. Two belt loops were sewn onto the back surface. A spare magazine was carried in the spine pocket and a combination screwdriver (Schraubenzieher) and magazine loader (Magazinfüller) could be found inside the holster flap. A cleaning rod was issued on the scale of one to every six guns[1].

The precise details of the holsters varied slightly, depending on where, when and by whom they had been made. Specimens may be found with their maker's name and date (ie: 'AWM/1/16', for AWM Sattlergenossenschaft, München, January 1916), and the mark of a Bekleidungsamt or clothing depot — 'B.A.XVIII.' being that of the 17th army corps. A few may even display the names of their owners.

The holster for the long-barrelled Pistole 08 was introduced in 1913[2], but was essentially a lengthened version of the standard Pistolentasche 08. It shared the distinctive 'bucket' flap, but its spine pouch contained a cleaning rod rather than an auxiliary magazine. These holsters were always issued with a wooden shoulder stock, a leather stock-retaining strap assembly, a leather boot to protect the tip of the stock (and hence the attachment mechanism), a leather carrying strap and a pouch containing two spare magazines. The holster was held to the stock by the carrying strap, which passed through slots in the wood; by the leather circlet to which the 'boot' was riveted; and by a strap, riveted to the stock body, which passed around the stock-butt and down over the holster flap. A strap on the holster body ran up through a loop stitched onto the lower part of the flap-leather and slipped over a stud on the stock-strap. LP 08 holsters now found with the studs affixed directly to the flaps are believed to have been converted after 1918 for the commercial market[3].

M.G.K.1.R.25.18.

Two examples of the Pistolentasche 08, dating from the First World War. **Left:** *made by Danziger Leder-Industrie in 1916 and bearing the marks of the clothing depot of 17th army corps.* **Right:** *made by Otto Sindel of Berlin in 1915, with the marks of the machine-gun company of 25th infantry regiment.*

B.A.XVII.

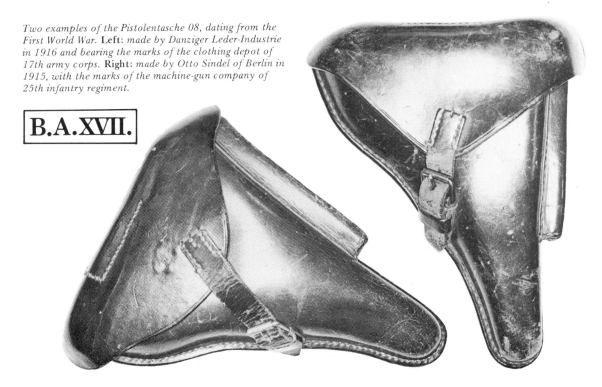

In addition, a number of accessories often accompanied the LP 08 — including the drum magazine (Trommelmagazin 08, TM 08) and its loading tool, dust cover and linen or leather container.

The C 96 was issued in a hollow wood-bodied holster-stock, retained in a special leather harness consisting of a leather plate linking a boot to a large collar. The protecting flap and retaining circlet for the cleaning rod, a pocket for the dismantling tool and the holster-stock retaining strap were all attached to the large upper collar. Two loops for a carrying strap lay on the back of the leather harness. Unit and military inspectors' marks were generally applied on the holster-stock body, while the back of the harness often bore its maker's name.

Notes

1. According to the official handbook for the P 08, published in 1909.

2. Sometimes — erroneously — called the 'Pistolentasche 13'.

3. John Walter, *Luger*, pp. 151-2, fails to make this point clear.

Key — 1, the pin punch carried in most Parabellum holsters; 2, the lang Pistole 08 holster; 3, an LP 08 holster made by Moritz Stecher of Freiberg in 1918, shortened after 1919 and fitted with a moulded tip; 4, a Pistole 08 in its holster, made by Lieferungsgenossenschaft der Sattler of Nürnberg in 1917. Note the magazine pouch and the pocket for the pin-punch. 5, the LP 08 shoulder stock; 6, the P 08 O-ring cleaning rod; 7 the naval P 04 rod; and 8, the rod for the LP 08. (1,6,7,8, Rolf Gminder; 2,5 Masami Tokoi.)

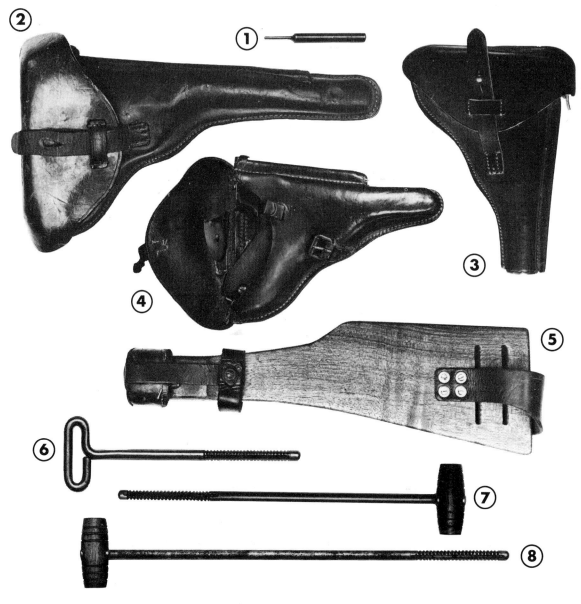

Table six
Holster manufacturers
Second Reich

Explanatory note

The list that follows contains fragmentary details of leatherware specialists known or suspected to have made holsters during the Second Reich. The data have been reconstructed from a number of sources and gaps inevitably remain. Corrections or further information will be welcomed by the author.

Wilhelm Schmidt (Berlin, f1835 d1947) sp — P LP M du.

company name

location, and dates of operation where known — 'f' is date of foundation, 'd' date of demise

Spelling of name questionable, unconfirmed or possibly incomplete

Types of holster known or suspected to have been made — 'P' for Pistole 08, 'LP' for lang Pistole 08, 'MP' for naval Pistole 04, 'M' for Mauser C 96, 'RR' for commission-designed revolvers

'Date of holster uncertain' which means that the company may not have been active prior to 1918, but that there is sufficient doubt to include it on the list

Albrecht & Noll (Berlin) sp — P.
Armee- & Marinehaus (Berlin, f1911? d1945?) — P LP MP.
Julius Arnade (Metz) sp — P.
Richard Appel (Frankfurt am Main) — P.
AWM Sattlergenossenschaft (München) — P LP.
Barney & Co. (Berlin) sp — P du.
Karl Barth (Waldbröl/Rheinland) — P du.
H(?). Becker (Berlin) sp — P du.
Carl Biller (Billess?) (Spandau) sp — P.
Böttcher & Renner (Nürnberg, f1901) — P.
Wilhelm Brand (Heidelberg, f1900) — P?
Briegl & Schneider (Ohrdruf in Thüringen) sp — P du.
Gustav Buchmüller (Stuttgart, f1831 d1961) — P?
A. & E. Buhler (Bühler?) (Stuttgart) sp — P?
N. Burghard (München-Pasing) — P.
Hans Clemen (Elberfeld) sp — P du.
Franz Cobau (Berlin-Reinickendorf, f pre-1908) — P du.
A. Dahl (Barmen, d1920s) — P.
F.J. Daniel (Bühl in Baden) — P, LP?
Hans Deuter (Augsburg, f1898) — P?
Wilh. Dopheide (Brackwede) sp — P.
J.M. Eckart (Ulm/Donau) — P du.
Chr. Ehlers (Kiel) — MP.
L. Estelmann (location unknown) sp — P.
Johann Fockler (Berlin) sp — P du.
Fritz Grosse (Dresden-Radebeul) sp — P du.
Carl Heinichen (Dresden) — P M.
Heinrich, Sohn (Neu-Ulm, f1871) — P?
Carl Henkel (Bielefeld, f1868?) — P?
Franz Herrmann (Erfurt) sp — P du.
Hohmann & Sohn (Kaiserslautern, f c.1890 d1938) — P du.
Arn. Hoffmann (Berlin) sp — P?
C. (G.?) Holste (München) sp — P.
Julius Jansen (Strassburg in Elsass) — RR, P.
S. Kellendorfer (München) sp — P du.
Kern, Kläger & Co. (Neu-Ulm, d1959) — P du.
Kleinheinz Lederwarenfabrik (München) sp — P du.
Herm. F. Kohr (Köln) sp — P du.
R. Kuhlewein & Co. (Erfurt) sp — P du.
Reinhold Kuhn (location unknown) sp — P du.
Leder-Schuler-Werke (Hamburg-Altona, f1838) — P? MP?
LGHR (Leipzig) — P du.
Lieferungsgenossenschaft der Sattler (LGS) (Nürnberg, f1915 d1969) — P LP RR.
Lieferungs-Verband von Mitglieder der Berliner Sattlerinnung, (Berlin and München) sp — P.
Ferd. Litzmann (Erzingen/Schwarzwald) sp — P du.
Loh & Söhne AG (Berlin) — P du.
Meier & Abitzsch (Leipzig) sp — P du.
Josef Moll (Goch/Rheinland f pre-1915 d1978) — P du.
Wilhelm Möller (Hameln, f1869) — P? du.
Muhlenfeld & Co. (Barmen and München?) sp — P du.
Albert Müller (Düsseldorf) — P.
Max G. Müller (Nürnberg, f1887? d1968) — P du.
Reinhard Nagel (Nagele?) & Co. (Bielefeld and Berlin, d1937) sp — P du.
Oberpfalzisch Lieferungs-Verband (Regensburg) sp — P du.
Max Oswald (Karlsruhe, f1910? d1945/6?) — P.
G. Passier & Sohn (Hannover, f1867) — P?
Perina & Co. (Hannover?) sp — P.
Hugo Pretzel & Co. (Berlin) — P.
Gustav Reinhardt (Berlin) — P.
Julius Richter (Dresden) sp — P du.
A. Ricke (Kassel, d1925?) sp — P.
L. Ritgen (Karlsruhe, f1870 d1944?) — P?
Ferd. Ritzman(n) (Neu-Ulm, d1945?) sp — P du.
C. A. Roever (Magdeburg) sp — P du.
Hans Römer (Neu-Ulm, f1871) — P du.
Carl Ruther (Berlin) sp — P du.
Ryffel & Borns (Hannover-Kirchrode, f1886) — P du.
Sattler- & Polsterer-Werkgenossenschaft (Berlin) sp — P du.
Sattlerei-Genossenschaft (Breslau) — P du.
Sattlerinnung Eisleben (Eisleben) — P du.
Saupe & Scherf (Chemnitz) sp — P du.
Schäfer & Reiche (Leipzig) sp — P du.
A. Scheidbrand(t?) (Bensberg) sp — P du.
Friedrich Scheuermann (Offenbach am Main, f pre-1900) — P.

TABLE SIX **2**

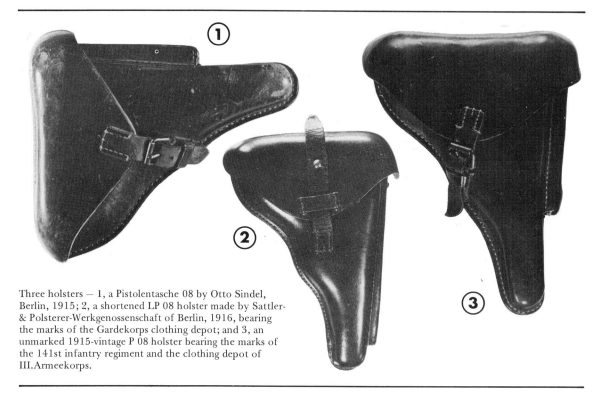

Three holsters — 1, a Pistolentasche 08 by Otto Sindel,
Berlin, 1915; 2, a shortened LP 08 holster made by Sattler-
& Polsterer-Werkgenossenschaft of Berlin, 1916, bearing
the marks of the Gardekorps clothing depot; and 3, an
unmarked 1915-vintage P 08 holster bearing the marks of
the 141st infantry regiment and the clothing depot of
III.Armeekorps.

Table seven
Holster makers' histories

Brief details of some — but by no means all — of the
leatherware makers known to have made holsters for the
Reichsrevolvers and the Parabellums prior to 1918. The
author would appreciate further details.
Key to holster production RR, Reichsrevolver; MP, naval
Parabellum; AP, Pistole 08; and LP, lang Pistole 08. Solid
symbols indicate observed production.

Albrecht & Noll. Berlin; working during the First World
War. Nothing is known about this leatherware manufacturer (?), the marks of which have been reported on
Parabellum holsters (WOL 1). No details can be traced
in the Berlin commercial directories and it is assumed that
trading ceased during the first years of the Weimar
Republic. *Trademark:* none known.

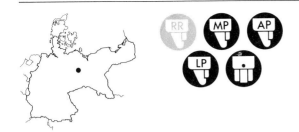

Armee- & Marinehaus, Inh. Deutscher-Offizier-Verein.
Berlin-Charlottenburg, Hardenbergstrasse in 1941; working
in the period 1911-45. This establishment succeeded the
'Warenhaus für Armee und Marine' shortly before the
outbreak of the First World War and traded until the
Russians overran Berlin in 1945. There is no evidence
that operations continued into the postwar era. The
Armee- & Marinehaus was a retailer of military goods
though small-scale manufacturing facilities may also have
been maintained. Uniforms, holsters, edged weapons, etc.,
have been recorded with the company's marks, which
included the letter code 'jme' granted in September 1941;
premises were then being occupied at Hardenbergstrasse
24. However, it is thought that a move from central Berlin
had occurred in the mid 1920s. *Trademark:* none known.

Julius Arnade. Metz (?), Département Moselle, France;
working during the First World War. Little is known about
this leatherware manufacturer, who reportedly made
Parabellum holsters for the German army before Alsace-
Lorraine was returned to France in 1919. Costanzo (WOL
1) records the town-name as 'Mats', but is probably wrong.
Trademark: none known.

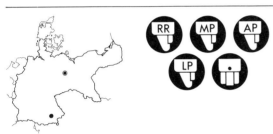

AWM Sattlergenossenschaft. München; working in the
1900-18 period and possibly much earlier. Very little is
known about this holster and military leatherware manufacturer, the marks of which have been found on commission revolver and Parabellum holsters made between
1899 and 1917. No further information has yet been
elicited from München's commercial registers and it is
concluded that the company failed to survive the early
years of the Weimar Republic, when there was little need
of its wares. *Trademark:* AWM.

F(ritz?). Bierenbrier. Kehl am Rhein; working during the
First World War. The name of this leatherware maker has
been reported on Parabellum and other pistol holsters
dating from the 1915-18 era. Various spellings of the name
have been attempted (WOL1, LHG, etc.) and the factory
has been placed in Suhl, Kiel and elsewhere. It was actually
sited at Kehl in the Rheinland, on the east bank of the
Rhine facing Strasbourg. Operations are believed to have
ceased in 1919, though substantiation is currently lacking.
Trademark: none known.

Carl Billess (possibly Biller), Lederwarenfabrik. Spandau;
working prior to 1918. The name of this holster maker
remains uncertain, since it has been listed elsewhere as
'Biller' or 'Billep'; these variations, it is assumed, have
arisen from confusing the fraktur Eszett (ß) with P or R.
No company of even similar name could be traced in the
Berlin registers and it is concluded that trading ceased
shortly after the end of the First World War. *Trademark:*
none known.

TABLE SEVEN **2**

 **A.F. Buhler** (Bühler?). Stuttgart; working during the First World War. Nothing is known about this leatherware-making business, the marks of which have been found on German Parabellum holsters made in 1915-16. No trace of Buhler has yet been found in the Stuttgart commercial directories and it is concluded that trading ceased during the early years of the Weimar Republic. *Trademark:* none known.

 **Hans Clemen**, Lederwarenfabrik. Elberfeld; working prior to 1918. Nothing is known of this company, a leatherware manufacturer reportedly involved in Parabellum holster production during the First World War. No details have yet been found in the Wuppertal-Elberfeld commercial directories, and it is assumed that trading ceased in the depression of the early 1920s. *Trademark:* none known.

 **A. Dahl**. Barmen; working in the early twentieth century. Very little is known about this leatherware maker, whose stamp has been found on Parabellum holsters dating from 1915-18. No information could be obtained from the Wuppertal-Elberfeld chamber of commerce and it is believed, therefore, that Dahl ceased trading in the early 1920s. *Trademark:* none known.

 **F.J. Daniel**. Bühl in Baden; working in 1910? Few details have come to light concerning this leatherware maker, the marks of whom have been reported on a holster for the Pistole 04 (naval Parabellum) believed to date from about 1910 and bearing marks of the 'LZA Strassburg'. Daniel was at one time believed to have operated in Suhl, though his actual location was Bühl — a small town in Baden, about 30km east north-east of Strasbourg (known to the pre-1919 Germans as Strassburg in Elsass but subsequently returned to France). Nothing has been heard since the end of the First World War and it is concluded that trading ceased in the early 1920s. *Trademark:* none known.

 **Danziger Leder-Industrie** (AG?). Danzig; working during the First World War. Little is yet known about this leatherware-making business, the marks of which have been reported on holsters dating from 1915-16 for the Pistole 08 and other German handguns. It is possible that operations continued through the Weimar Republic and the Third Reich until the end of the Second World War, but no leather goods have been conclusively identified from these periods and the theory remains unproven. Danzig is now Gdansk in Poland and obtaining details remains extremely difficult. *Trademark:* none known.

 **Deutsche Signalflaggenfabrik GmbH**. Karlsruhe in Baden; working during the First World War. This maker of signal-flags and leather or canvas goods — including bayonet frogs and possibly holsters — is believed to have been founded in about 1895. Its operations seem to have ceased immediately after the end of the First World War and, consequently, little else is known. *Trademark:* two flags in saltire(?).

Wilh. Dopheide. Brackwede; working from c.1915 until 1943. Little is known about this maker of holsters, bayonet frogs and other military items during the First World War and the Third Reich, except that he seems to have been superseded by Heinrich Dopheide during the Second World War. *Trademark:* none known.

J.M. Eckart, Lederwarenfabrik. Ulm/Donau (sometimes wrongly placed in Köln); working 1913-46. This leather-ware manufacturing company is known to have made Parabellum holsters during the second decade of the twentieth century — the earliest known example, issued to the 2nd dragoon regiment, dating from 1913 — and the Third Reich. Eckart received the code letters 'dyo' in April 1941, but is believed to have ceased trading at or shortly after the end of the Second World War. No further details have been obtained from commercial records in Ulm. *Trademark:* none known.

Chr. Ehlers Lederwarenfabrik. Kiel; working during the First World War. Little is known about this leatherware manufacturer, whose marks have been found on holsters for the naval Parabellum and belt frogs for naval cutlasses. The Kiel chamber of commerce reports that Ehlers is no longer in existence but, at the time of writing, it is not known whether trading ceased during the early years of the Weimar Republic or at the end of the Second World War. *Trademark:* none known.

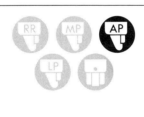

Friedrich, Erben. Berlin; working prior to 1920? The identification of this holster maker remains uncertain, as the company name has been filed as 'Erb' rather than Friedrich. Erben means 'successors' in English and the trading style could consequently be written as 'successors to Friedrich'. The era in which it operated is also uncon-firmed but seems likely to have been the Second Reich rather than the Third; trading may have ceased in the economic depression of the early 1920s. *Trademark:* none known.

C. Holste & Companie. München; working during the First World War and possibly later. Very few details of this leatherware manufacturer have come to light, though Parabellum holsters are known to have been made in 1917-18. The München chamber of commerce reports that Holste no longer exists but it is not known if trading ceased during the depression of the early 1920s or at the end of the Second World War. NB: the company name has also been recorded as 'G. Holste' and the correct form has not been adequately established. *Trademark:* none known.

TABLE SEVEN **4**

Julius Jansen. Strassburg in Elsass; working during the Second Reich. This maker of saddlery and leatherware operated in Strasbourg in Alsace-Lorraine, the French provinces occupied by the Germans from 1871 until the end of the First World War. Jansen's marks have been found on holsters destined for the 1883-pattern German commission revolver (dated 1895-1908), some of which were converted in 1908-9 for the first Parabellums. Little else is known and it is assumed that trading ceased in about 1920 — though operations may have continued after Strasbourg had been returned to French control. *Trademark:* none known.

Two views of a 1905-vintage Jansen-made M 1891 revolver holster, modified for the Pistole 08 in c.1908.

Lieferungsgenossenschaft der Sattler (LGS). Nürnberg; founded in 1915 and dissolved in 1969. This union of otherwise insignificant leatherware makers was founded during the First World War — on 3rd March 1915 — and is known to have handled all kinds of military articles, including Parabellum holsters, cartridge pouches, bayonet frogs and belts. *Trademark:* LGS.

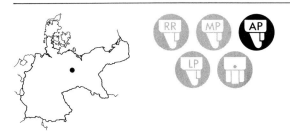

Lieferungs-Verband von Mitglieder der Berliner Sattlerinnung. Berlin and München; working during the First World War. This organisation — its name means 'delivery association of the members of the Berlin saddlers guild' — was formed during the First World War to facilitate the supply of leather goods such as saddles, ammunition pouches and holsters to the German armies. Holsters have been seen dated 1916-18. The association was based in Berlin, but a depot in München served the needs of the Bavarian army. Its operations ceased shortly after 1918. *Trademark:* LVMBS.

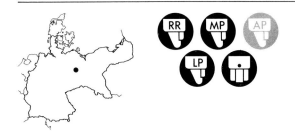

Loh Söhne AG. Berlin; working during the First World War and possibly later. Very little is known about this leatherware-making company, the marks of which have been found on holsters for the three German Parabellums — standard, 'artillery' and naval — made in 1912-18. The stampings generally read 'Loh Söhne Act.Ges./Berlin', though a variation reading 'Loh & Söhne' is said to exist. No details have been extracted from the Berlin directories and it is concluded that trading ceased during the Weimar Republic. *Trademark:* none known.

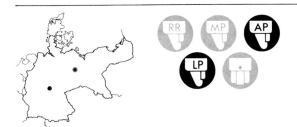 **Maury & Companie.** Offenbach am Main, Luisenstrasse; founded prior to 1915 and working until 1960. Maury was allocated the code letters 'hlv' in August 1941, when trading from Luisenstrasse 16, but is also known to have made holsters for the Pistolen and langen Pistolen 08 (standard and 'artillery' Parabellums) during the First World War. The company entered the commercial register on 27th April 1918 and was finally liquidated on 28th July 1960. *Trademark:* none known.

 **Muhlenfeld & Companie.** Barmen (and München?); working during the First World War. The name of this leatherware manufacturer has been reported on Parabellum holsters dating from 1915-18, though the location of the factory is a little uncertain; no traces of the company could be found in the commercial registers in Wuppertal-Elberfeld or München, however, and it must be assumed that trading has long ceased. *Trademark:* possibly MM.

 **Albert Müller.** Düsseldorf; working during the First World War. Nothing has yet been discovered about this leatherware manufacturer, known to have made holsters for the 1904-pattern naval Parabellum in 1917-18. No records could be traced in Düsseldorf and it is concluded that trading ceased during the early years of the Weimar Republic. *Trademark:* none known.

 **Perina & Companie, Lederwarenfabrik.** Hannover (?); working during the First World War. The marks of this leatherware maker have been reported on Parabellum holsters dated between 1915 and 1917. Perina is believed to have operated in Hannover, but no information could be extracted from the city's commercial directories or archives and the claim should consequently be treated as suspect. *Trademark:* none known.

 **Gustav Reinhardt.** Berlin; working between 1914 and 1945. Little is known about this leatherware-making company, the marks of which have been found on Parabellum and other holsters dating from the First World War and the Third Reich. Reinhardt was granted the code letters 'jsd' in September 1941, when trading was being undertaken at 'Berlin SW68, Brandenburg-strasse 72-73' according to the code books, but nothing else is known. The firm is no longer in existence. *Trademark:* none known.

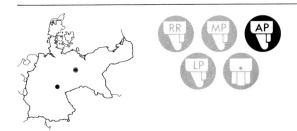 **A. Ricke Lederwarenfabrik.** Cassel; working in the 1915-18 era. Few details of this leatherware-making business have yet been extracted from records in Karlsruhe. A few holsters destined for the Pistole 08 (Parabellum) have been examined from the First World War period, but the absence of Ricke from Karlsruhe directories for 1925-30 suggests that trading ceased very shortly after the hostilities had done so. Nothing else is yet known. *Trademark:* none.

TABLE SEVEN **6**

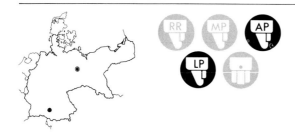

Hans Römer GmbH & Companie. Neu-Ulm, Arnulfstrasse; founded in 1871. This leatherware manufacturer registered with the local chamber of commerce in 1929, but holsters for the Parabellum and other handguns — including the Pistole 08 and the long or 'artillery' model — have been identified from the 1917-18 period and it is clear that business was established a decade or more prior to registry. Military equipment was made during the Third Reich, when Römer, described as a 'Fabrik für Heeresaurüstung' in the codebooks, was allocated the code-group 'bml' (February 1941). Holsters, cartridge pouches, map cases, belts and saddlery have been reported from 1935-45, but operations are currently concentrated on camping articles, safety seats, and crash- and protective helmets. *Trademark:* none known.

Friedrich Scheuermann. Offenbach am Main and Frankfurt am Main; founded prior to 1900. This leatherware maker entered the Offenbach commercial register on 2nd January 1900 and has been identified as a producer of Parabellum holsters during the First World War and the Third Reich. The company worked in Offenbach until April 1956 when it moved to Frankfurt; Goethestrasse 35 was its last known Offenbach address. *Trademark:* none known.

Otto Sindel, Militäreffekten- & Lederwarenfabrik. Berlin-Ost, Holzmarktstrasse, in 1941; working in the 1914-45 period. This manufacturer of military articles and leather goods is known to have made holsters for the Parabellum during the First World War (1915-17 noted) and the Third Reich (1934-41), the latter for police or military use. Holsters for handguns of other types, bayonet frogs, map cases, cartridge pouches and other items have also been seen with Sindel's marks — which included the code 'cvb', allocated in March 1941 when a factory was being operated at Holzmarktstrasse 67 in 'Berlin O27', Trading is believed to have ceased at or shortly after the end of the Second World War. *Trademark:* none known.

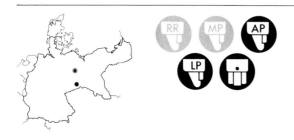

Moritz Stecher, Lederwarenfabrik. Freiberg Bezirks Dresden; working 1918-44/5. This leatherware-making company is known to have produced holsters for the langen Pistolen 08 (1918), the Pistolen 08 (1918 and 1936-9), belts, cartridge pouches and other military articles. The code letters 'jwa' were granted in September 1941 but have yet to be found on a P 08 holster. Stecher traded in a small town 30km south-west of Dresden — not in Lower Saxony, near Hamburg, as had once been thought — but few other details have yet been obtained and trading may have ceased in the last stages of the Second World War. *Trademark:* none known.

TABLE SEVEN **7**

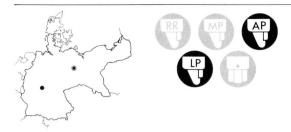

Stern & Companie. Offenbach am Main; working during the First World War. The marks of this leatherware manufacturer have been found on holsters for the standard and long ('artillery') Parabellums, all dating from 1918. Nothing has yet been discovered in the Offenbach or Frankfurt directories and it is concluded that the company ceased trading during the early years of the Weimar Republic. *Trademark:* possibly a distinctive star, 'Stern' in German.

Vereinigte Fabrikanten für Militärlederzeuge GmbH. Solingen; working during the First World War. No information about this combine, believed to have been a group of unimportant leatherware makers working together to honour military contracts, has yet been forthcoming from archives in Solingen; trading may have ceased in 1918, whereafter the participants probably continued operations individually. Parabellum and other holsters have been identified with the Vereinigte Fabrikanten's marks. *Trademark:* S in a triangle.

A. Wunderlich Nachfolger. Berlin and Berlin-Neukölln; founded in the 1890s (?) and trading until 1945 or later. Little is yet known about this leatherware manufacturer, founded in the late nineteenth century but sold to Wunderlich's successor (Nachfolger — 'Nf.' or 'Nachf.') by 1912/13. Holsters for the Parabellum and other guns were made during the early 1900s (1913-18 noted), the Weimar Republic and the Third Reich. The factory moved from Berlin SW to the south-eastern suburbs of Neukölln in about 1937. *Trademark:* none known.

TABLE SEVEN **8**

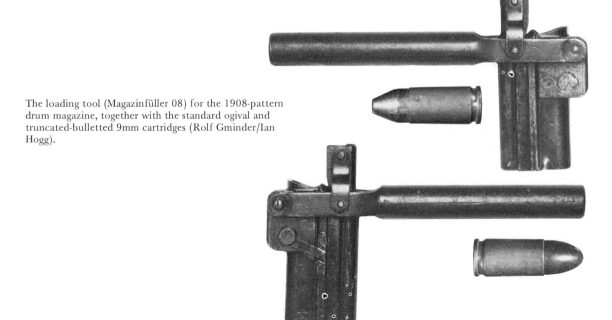

The loading tool (Magazinfüller 08) for the 1908-pattern drum magazine, together with the standard ogival and truncated-bulletted 9mm cartridges (Rolf Gminder/Ian Hogg).

PART FIVE

The ammunition

The standard cartridge for the M 79 and M 83 revolvers was developed in the late 1870s – possibly by Gebrüder Mauser & Co., or, equally possibly, by the committee responsible for the original revolver.

Developed at a time when 'shocking power' was of paramount importance, the ball cartridge (Scharfen Patrone) is very typical of its era. The large lead bullet, cylindrical with an ogival nose, had a diameter of about 10.87±0.22mm, a weight of 17±0.15gm, and two exposed cannelures containing the barrel lubricant. This was a mixture of five parts beeswax and one of paraffin. The straight brass case, about 24.7±0.2mm long, was crimped into the bullet immediately behind the rearmost cannelure and contained a charge of Neues Gewehrpulver 71 ('new rifle powder'). The charge initially weighed 1.5gm, but was reduced to 1.35gm in 1885 in anticipation of the introduction of the short-barrelled M 83 revolver. There were several cartridge case-heads, including an old folded, a new solid, and Mauser 'A' base types. The cases were generally Berdan primed. The loaded rounds weighed about 24gm, measured 36-38mm overall, and attained a muzzle velocity of between 200 and 205mps. The muzzle energy of about 35kgm was inferior to that of the 9mm Parabellum, but the heavy large-diameter lead bullets were much better man stoppers.

Blank and drill cartridges (Platz- und Exerzierpatronen) were also developed. The former consisted of a standard primed and charged case loaded with a papier-mâché or hollow wooden bullet, while the latter had a dummy 'bullet' – little more than a brass shell – riveted into the primerless case. An auxiliary practice device may also be encountered. This comprises a rimmed solid brass or steel cylinder, with a pocket in the base for a primer and a hemispherical depression in the nose for a small lead ball. The primer was sufficiently powerful to propel the ball accurately to distances of 20 metres or more.

The 9mm Parabellum cartridge, which chambered in all military Parabellum pistols, was officially designated 'Patrone für Pistolen Parabellum 08' prior to 1934. It was developed from the 7.65mm Parabellum cartridge and has since become the world's most famous pistol and machine-carbine round. It was designed in response to army doubts about the man-stopping qualities of the smaller 7.65mm bullet, and provided a heavier, larger-diameter projectile travelling at comparable velocity. In early 1902, Luger and DWM experimented with slightly-necked cases and unusually blunt nose bullets, but development continued in the Berlin research bureau until a straight case had been perfected. The 7.65mm and 9mm Parabellum cartridges shared the same case-rim and case-head dimensions, which meant that pistols could be chambered for either round simply by changing the barrel. The breech-face and extractor designs were common to both.

Few alterations were made to the basic 9mm Parabellum design during the First World War, but, in about 1916, nickel in the bullet jacket was replaced by copper. The experiment was not especially successful, and nickel was reintroduced in 1918 although copper was available in greater quantities. The original truncated bullet was replaced in 1917 by an ogival pattern*, which eliminated the feed problems of the Trommelmagazine or drum magazines, issued with the 'artillery' Parabellums and the Bergmann machine carbine.

Issue of both bullet types continued until the Armistice; the truncated variety was used only with the standard Parabellum box magazines – in theory, if not always in practice. Most German 9mm cartridges had black primer annuli.

*The truncated pattern was declared contrary to the Hague convention; additionally, the ogival pattern fed better from the drum magazine.

Typical headstamps: 10·6mm

1, manufacturer's code letter(s); 2, month of delivery; 3, year of delivery; 4, brass material mark.

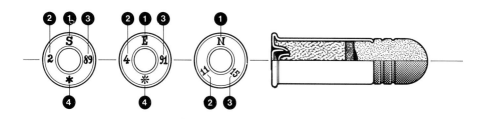

A number of different blank (Platzpatrone), drill (Exerzierpatrone) and special-purpose cartridges were developed. A high pressure test round (Beschuss Patrone) gave 75% more pressure than normal and was used for proof firing: some rounds are simply headstamped 'Beschuss', but others bear normal headstamps with either green primer annuli or green-lacquered case-heads. They should never be fired in conditions other than laboratory tests.

At least one pistol was adapted for a Maxim-pattern silencer in 1916, and special cartridges were made in small numbers. These short-range Nahpatronen used standard DWM 480C cases, but the propellant charge was reduced from 0.36gm to 0.25gm and the bullet weight was increased from 8gm to 9gm. This ensured subsonic velocity, below 345mps, but the bullet was only accurate to about 100m. This, and the modifications required to achieve semi-automatic operation, caused the project to be abandoned.

Typical headstamps: 9mm

1, manufacturer's code letter(s); 2, month of delivery; 3, year of delivery; 4, 'reload' mark.

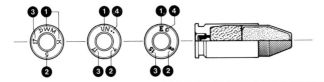

Table eight **cartridge manufacturers**

1, Revolver-Patrone; 2, 9mm Parabellum, truncated bullet; 3, 9mm Parabellum, ogival bullet; and 4, 7.65mm Parabellum (commercial). Solid symbols indicate known production.

Only a handful of contractors has yet been identified with the production of 9mm Parabellum cartridges in the period 1908-18, most of them being recruited during the First World War. In addition, the interpretation of some code-letters remains suspect; indeed, it seems possible that marks applied to 9mm pistol and 7.9mm rifle ammunition did not mean the same thing. Consequently, two different companies may have used the same code-letter, but on different cartridges.

C

C. Patronenfabrik Cassel (also wrongly identified with 'Patronenfabrik Cleebronn, Württemberg'). This establishment made standard 9mm cartridges, loaded with ogival bullets, in 1917-18.

D

D. Königlich sächsisches Patronenfabrik, Dresden, Saxony (also wrongly identified with 'Patronenfabrik Danzig'). Cartridges were made here from 1909 until the end of the First World War, a change from truncated to ogival bullets occurring in 1916.

DWM K
DM

DWM K. Deutsche Waffen- & Munitionsfabriken AG, Karlsruhe, Baden. DWM supplied the army with large numbers of rounds bearing standard commercial headstamps in 1908, and then made standard military-stamped items until the end of the First World War. Bullets changed from truncated to ogival in 1916.

E, Ɛ
Ɛ̲

E. Königlich Munitionsfabrik, Erfurt, Thüringen. Parabellum ammunition seems to have been made from 1909 until the end of the First World War. The 'E' mark may be in script.

Ge D **GD**		*G D or Ge D.* Gustav Genschow & Co. AG, Durlach bei Karlsruhe, Baden. This company, which produced 9mm ammunition only in the period 1915-18, can be confused with 'GE' – Georg Egerstorff of Hannover-Linden.
H		*H.* Believed to be Hirtenberg Patronen-, Zündhütchen- & Metallwarenfabrik, Hirtenberg, Austria; though also identified with 'Hein. Hück & Co., Nürnberg' and 'Rheinische Metallwarenfabrik, Düsseldorf'.
J		*J.* Hauptlaboratorium Ingolstadt, Ingolstadt, Bavaria; 1911-14 only?
L		*L.* Lindener Zündhütchen- & Patronenfabrik AG. Linden bei Hannover. This company, purchased by Dynamit AG vormals Alfred Nobel & Co. in 1927, made Parabellum cartridges in 1918.
MWs **MW**		*MW.* Munitionswerke Schönebeck, Schönebeck an der Elbe (later owned by Sellier & Bellot). This factory made 9mm pistol rounds in 1916-18.
RM		*RM.* Rheinische Metallwaren- & Maschinenfabrik AG, Sömmerda, Saxony ('Rheinmetall'). 9mm Parabellum cartridges were made between 1915 and the end of the First World War.
S		*S.* Königlich Munitionsfabrik, Spandau. This government-owned arsenal, one of the original prewar contractors, made 9mm ammunition from 1909 until 1918.
UN		*UN.* Heinrich Utendörffer & Co., Nürnberg. Utendörffer had been acquired by Rheinisch-Westfälische Sprengstoff ('RWS') in 1889, but traded under its original name until the end of the First World War. Parabellum rounds were made in 1917-18 only.
88		*88.* This monogram is believed to have belonged to Oberschlesische Eisenwerke AG, later bought by Hugo Schneider AG ('HASAG'). 9mm ammunition was made in 1917-18.

TABLE EIGHT **2**

Right: a comparison of cartridges. From the left – 6.35mm ACP, 7.65mm ACP, 7.65mm Parabellum; 7.63mm Mauser, 9mm Short and 9mm Parabellum (Ian Hogg).

PART SIX

The markings

Pistols issued to the Germans often bear unit markings on their butt caps and grip straps. Fewer Parabellums will be found these with marks, as most of them were made and issued during the war — when the time spent applying the unit designations, painstakingly, letter by letter and number by number, was used to repair and service front-line weapons. However, because the markings can identify the formations in which the guns served (and there may be more than one), a marked gun is infinitely more interesting than a plain one.

According to the 1909 marking regulations, the *Vorschrift über das Stempeln der Handwaffen,* there were three official punch sizes: 2.1mm, 3.1mm and 4.2mm being the heights of the capital letters. These were applied as:

4.2mm (capitals), 2.5mm (lower case): the unit type.
3.1mm: the individual unit number, and the company, battalion or column number.
2.1mm: the weapon number.

These were applied to the butt cap, the separately carried ejecting rod and the screwdriver of the Revolver M 79, and on the backstrap of the Revolver M 83 directly behind the lanyard ring. Parabellums were usually marked on the front grip-strap, running upwards toward the trigger guard.

The unit markings are, admittedly, extremely confusing; there were several important handbooks governing their application, and some letters changed their meaning from one book to another. The most important regulations were published in 1877, 1909 (1910 in Bavaria) and — after the First World War — in 1923 and 1934. And each was constantly revised by the issue of printed amendments, or Deckblätter. The result was a very complicated system in which some knowledge of the structure of the German army was necessary to distinguish apparently identical or contradictory markings.

Very few attempts have been made in English to explain the marks and, even in Germany, only the 1877 handbook is readily available[1]. An effort has been made by William Chamberlain in the 1975 *Gun Collector's Digest,* but this is something of a simplification. It is, in any case, only based on the 1877 regulations. Typical of the confusion that can arise is the identification of the stamp 'B' as indicating a Bavarian unit; by the First World War, it could also mean 'Bekleidungsamt' (clothing depot), 'Bäckerei' (bakery) or 'Brückentrain' (bridging train). Similarly, 'E' represented 'Ersatz' in 1877, but by 1909 could also mean 'Eisenbahn' (railway). The significance of an ordinary and script 'R' (R and ℜ) also varied from book to book.

Considerable information can be drawn from these marks. In this way, '24.R.3.71.' indicates that the weapon was the 71st to be issued to the third company of the 24th infantry regiment — 'Infanterie-Regiment Grossherzog Friedrich Franz von Mecklenburg-Schwerin (4.Brandenburgisches) Nr. 24'. This unit, part of III. Armeekorps in 1914, was raised in 1813 and garrisoned in Neu-Ruppin. Its history and battle honours can be determined from army lists, lineages, campaign histories, etc. Similarly, 'B.5.A.5.51.' represents the fifth Bavarian field artillery regiment: 'Feldartillerie-Regiment König Alfons XIII von Spanien, Nr. 5', part of II. (Bayr.) Armeekorps in 1914, raised in 1890 and garrisoned in Landau.

Note

1. The 1877 markings handbook, *Vorschrift über das Bezeichnen und Numerien der. . .Waffen,* was reprinted by Jurgen Olmes, 'Heere der Vergangenheit', in his publication *Das Sponton* — 6 Jahrgang, 1966.

Table nine **Unit marks**

The following, taken from Parabellums in the Imperial War Museum collection, show the types of marks that may be found — and also indicate how many of them were not applied strictly in accordance with the official regulations.

B.12.R.9.3.

P 08, DWM, undated (1909), serial number 1696b. Applied in accordance with regulations: 12.Bayerisches Infanterie-Regiment Prinz Arnulf, 9th company, pistol number 3. This unit was raised in 1814, garrisoned in Neu-Ulm, and a part of I.Bayerisches Armeekorps in 1914.

P 08, DWM, 1916, 9233a. Not applied in accordance with the regulations, as it should read '109.R.10...': 1.Badisches Leib-Grenadier-Regiment Nr. 109, 10th company, no pistol number. The regiment was raised in 1803, garrisoned in Karlsruhe, and a part of XIV.Armeekorps in 1914.

GREN.R.109.10.

P 08, DWM, 1912, 9452. Not applied in accordance with the regulations, as it should read '8.R.M.G.3.': Leib-Grenadier-Regiment König Friedrich Wilhelm III (1.Brandenburgisches) Nr. 8, machine-gun company, pistol number 3. The regiment was raised in 1808, garrisoned in Frankfurt an der Oder, and a part of III.Armeekorps in 1914.

G.R.8.M.G.3.

P 08, DWM, 1910, 5179b. Not applied in accordance with the regulations, as it should read '12.J.1.12.': 1.königlich Sächsisches Jäger-Bataillon Nr. 12, 1st company, pistol number 12. This battalion was raised in 1809, garrisoned in Freiberg in Sachsen, and a part of XII.Armeekorps in 1914.

J.B.12.1.12.

P 08, DWM, 1913, 214b. Applied approximately in accordance with the regulations: königlich Sächsisches Schützen-(Füsilier-)Regiment Prinz Georg, Nr. 108, machine-gun troop attached to 7th company, pistol number 12. The regiment was raised in 1809, garrisoned in Dresden, and a part of XII.Armeekorps in 1914.

108.R.7.M.G.K.12.

P 08, DWM, 1911, 9152a. Applied in accordance with the regulations: Reserve-Ulanen-Regiment Nr. 5, 2nd squadron, pistol number 17.

5.ℛ.U.2.17.

P 08, Erfurt, 1913, 5912. Applied in accordance with the regulations: machine-gun company of the Garde-Schützen-Bataillon, pistol number 61. The battalion was raised in 1814, garrisoned in Berlin-Lichterfelde, and a part of the Gardekorps in 1914.

G.S.M.G.61.

P 08, DWM, 1910, 4581d. Applied in accordance with the regulations: Husaren-Regiment Königin Wilhelmina der Niederlände (Hannover'sches) Nr. 15, 5th squadron, pistol number 8. The regiment was raised in 1803, garrisoned in Wandsbek, and a part of XI.Armeekorps in 1914.

15.H.5.8.

P 08, DWM, 1917, 4170e. Not applied in accordance with regulations, as it should read '161.R.10.4.': 10.Rheinisches Infanterie-Regiment Nr. 161, 10th company, pistol number 4. The regiment was raised in 1897, garrisoned in Trier and Köln, and a part of VIII.Armeekorps in 1914. (Note the use of 'J' instead of 'I' for 'Infanterie'; this practice was widespread.)

J.R.161.10.4.

P 08, Erfurt, 1912, 124a. Applied in accordance with the regulations: 8.Württembergisches Infanterie-Regiment Grossherzog Friedrich von Baden, Nr. 126, 1st company, pistol number 28. The regiment was raised in 1716, garrisoned in Strassburg im Elsass, and a part of XIII.Armeekorps in 1914.

126.R.1.28.

P 08, DWM, 1910, 2844d. Applied in accordance with the regulations: Ulanen-Regiment von Schmidt (1.Pommersches) Nr. 4, 5th squadron, pistol number 2. The regiment was raised in 1815, garrisoned in Thorn, and a part of XVII. Armeekorps in 1914.

4.U.5.2.

P 08, DWM, 1915, 2363g. Applied approximately in accordance with the regulations: Reserve-Ersatz-Regiment Nr. 4, 3rd company, pistol number 4. This unit was formed after mobilisation in 1914.

R.E.R.4.3.4.

TABLE NINE 2

There were many other marks, but these are rarely found on the semi-automatic pistols — though they do occasionally appear on the older revolvers. The marks of the 'Ersatz' or substitute units generally paralleled those of the regular army, but contained an additional 'E'; typical of these were '27.R.10.25.' and '27.R.E.2.25.' the former being applied by the 10th company of Infanterie-Regiment Prinz Louis Ferdinand von Preussen (2.Magdeburgisches) Nr. 27, and the latter by the 2nd company of the Ersatz-Bataillon. In the words of German Order of Battle 1944, which still

applied so far as the substitute units were concerned:
'. . . every unit in the Field Army is affiliated for personnel replacement purposes with a specific unit of the Replacement Training Army. . .known as an Ersatz unit. The normal location of the Ersatz unit is the home station of the affiliated field unit, to which the soldiers expect ultimately to return for their discharge or reassignment. For example, a soldier who is wounded and goes to a reserve hospital in the rear echelon will be sent, on leaving the hospital, to his. . . Ersatz unit before being returned to the field.

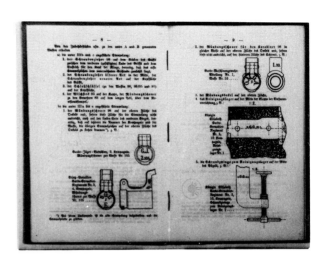

Markings handbook,
1909

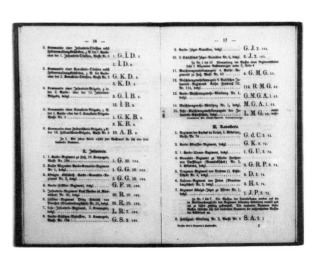

Very few Parabellums have been noted with 'Reserve' unit stamps, which generally included an additional script R — though, by the time of the 1909 regulations, this often replaced the standard R in markings such as those applied to infantry weapons. The stampings applied by Reserve-Infanterie-Regiment Nr. 29, therefore, would read '29.R.ℜ.10.25.' or simply '29.ℜ.10.25.'. M 79 and M 83 revolvers may also be encountered with Landwehr (an additional or replacement 'L') or Landsturm ('Ldst.' or 'ℒ') unit designations.

Directory of unit abbreviations

 MARKS A–ATA

A. This code letter, found in German unit markings, was applied by the field artillery regiments (Feldartillerie-Regimenter) under the regulations of 1877 and 1909. A typical mark reads '5.A.5.25.', for the 25th weapon issued to the 5th battery of Feldartillerie-Regiment Nr. 5. The following units existed in 1914: *Prussian regiments* — 1-11, 14-27, 30, 31, 33-47, 50-63, 66, 67, 69-76 and 79-84; *Saxon regiments* — 12, 28, 32, 48, 64, 68, 77 and 78; *Württemberg regiments* — 13, 29, 49 and 65.

A.B. This mark, applied under the 1909 regulations, was used by the Feldartillerie-Brigaden; thus, '10.A.B.25.' signified the 25th weapon issued to 10.Feldartillerie-Brigade.

A.E. This property mark was applied by the Ersatz-Batterien (supplementary batteries) of the Feldartillerie-Regimenter under the 1909 regulations. A typical example reads '5.A.E.1.25.', showing that the weapon was issued to the 1st supplementary battery of the 5th field artillery regiment.

A.E.r. This combination of code letters showed that the weapon on which it appeared had been issued to a supplementary mounted battery of a field artillery regiment (reitende Ersatz Batterie des Feldartillerie-Regiments). A typical example reads '5.A.E.r.1.25.'.

A.F. These letters were applied by the Fussartillerie-Regimenter, or foot artillery regiments. A typical specimen reads '15.A.F.3.45.' for the 45th weapon issued to the 3rd battery of the 15th foot artillery unit. There were twenty such regiments in August 1914, numbered from 1; all were Prussian except 12 and 19, raised in Saxony.

A.F.E. This combination of letter-marks was granted to the Ersatz-Bataillone des Fussartillerie-Regimenter (supplementary battalions of the foot artillery regiments) by the 1909 regulations. It takes the form '15.A.F.E.1.25.' for the 25th weapon issued to the first battery of the supplementary battalion of Fussartillerie-Regiment Nr.15.

A.F.H. or A.F...H. These three letters appeared in marks applied in the post-1909 period by relatively insignificant foot artillery units, munitions columns carrying supplies for Haubitzen (howitzers). They may usually be found stamped as '5.A.F.II.2.H.25.', the 25th weapon issued to the 2nd (howitzer) munitions column attached to II. Bataillon of Fussartillerie-Regiment Nr.5.

A.F.M. or A.F...M. These letters were granted to a relatively insignificant German foot artillery unit, an ammunition column carrying supplies for the mortars. See AFH for further details.

A.F.R. These were applied by the recruiting depots of foot artillery regiments (Rekrutendepots des Fussartillerie-Regiments) under the 1909 marking regulations, but are rarely encountered. A typical specimen reads '5.A.F.R.45.'.

A.M. These code letters were applied by the German Artillerie-Munitionskolonnen (artillery ammunition columns) prior to 1918. A typical example reads 'A.M.VI.3.25.', the 25th weapon issued to the 3rd ammunition column attached to VI.Armeekorps.

A.R. This code signified the recruiting depot of a field artillery regiment (Rekrutendepot des Feldartillerie-Regiments). It appeared as '5.A.R.45.'.

A.r. These code letters were used by the reitende Batterien (mounted batteries) of the German field artillery regiments, taking the form '10.A.r.2.25.'.

A.T.A. These markings, which appeared in the form of 'A.T.A.2.25.' with the T in script, signified the Armee-Telegraphen-Abteilungen or army telegraph units.

Directory **1**

 MARKS BA-BU

B.A. or B...A. Applied in the form of 'B.5.A.2.35.', this code group signified any of the twelve Bavarian field artillery regiments (Bayerisches Feldartillerie-Regimenter). It survived the revised 1909 regulations unchanged from 1877/8.

B.A. This mark, in the form of 'B.A.II.25.', is associated with the German army's clothing depots (Bekleidungs-ämter) — in this particular instance, that of the II.Armeekorps. It is rarely if ever found on Parabellums but often lies on Parabellum holsters.

B.A.F. or B...A.F. Marks such as 'B.2.A.F.2.25.' were used by the three Bavarian foot artillery regiments (Bayerisches Fussartillerie-Regimenter) from the 1870s until the end of the First World War.

B.Ch. or B...Ch. The Bavarian Chevauleger regiment ('light horse', a form of cavalry) applied marks of this type, a typical example reading 'B.5.Ch.2.35.'; there were eight such units in August 1914.

B.L. These code letters associated with the Bavarian Leib-Infanterie-Regiment, occasionally found on the grip straps of Parabellums in the form of 'B.L.5.45.' (or perhaps 'L.5.45.'). They may also be struck into holsters, etc.

B.M.G.A. or B...M.G.A. This represented the independent Bavarian machine-gun unit (Bayerische Maschinengewehr-Abteilung), and may often be found on Parabellums in the form of 'B.1.M.G.A.15.'.

B.P. or B...P. The Bavarian pioneer battalions (Bayerische Pionier Bataillone), four of which existed in August 1914, applied marks reading 'B.3.P.2.25.'; few will ever be found on Parabellums as second-rate weapons were usually carried.

B.R. This combination of code letters usually signified that the gun belonged to any of the 23 Bavarian infantry regiments extant in 1914; the marks read 'B.15.R.5.45.'

B.R.K. (R in script). This mark was associated with the three pre-1918 Bavarian reserve cavalry regiments, or Reserve-Kavallerie-Regimenter. Most of the examples examined were struck as 'B.2.R.K.3.35.', with a B-prefix for Bayerisches ('Bavarian').

B.R.M.G. or B...R.M.G. Marks of this type were applied under the 1909 regulations to weapons carried by the machine-gun companies attached to Bavarian infantry regiments, twenty-three of which existed in August 1914. The stampings generally took the form of 'B.15.R.M.G. 25.', but a few non-standard variations have been seen.

B.s.R. or B...s.R. (R in script). This mark was used by the two Bavarian Schweres Reiter-Regimenter, heavy cavalry units, in the form 'B.1.s.R.2.25.'. It survived the 1909 regulations unchanged from the 1870s.

B.U. or B...U. The two Bavarian Ulanen-Regimenter (lancers) used unit markings of this type, applied as 'B.1.U.2.25.' to pistols and their accessories.

Ch. This unit mark was associated with the Bavarian light cavalry regiments (Chevauleger-Regimenter). See B.Ch.

D. This code letter, introduced by the 1877 regulations and remaining unaltered by the 1909 revisions, was applied to weapons and equipment used by the dragoon (Dragoner) regiments, 26 of which existed in August 1914 — *Prussia*: 1-24; *Württemberg*: 25-6. It may be encountered in the form of '5.D.2.25.', though a few non-standard variations have been reported.

 MARKS E-EMGK

E. This often appeared in German unit markings — whether applied under the 1877 regulations or the revised code of 1909 — as an abbreviated form of 'Ersatz' (substitute). In most cases it supplemented a normal mark: '25.R.E.2.35.', for example, represented the Ersatz-Bataillon of an infantry regiment.

E. This code letter sometimes appears on German weapons and equipment, an abbreviated form of 'Eisenbahn' (railway).

E.M.G. These pre-1918 German property marks were applied by the Ersatz-Maschinengewehr-Kompagnien, or supplementary machine-gun companies, in the guise of '1.E.M.G.35.'. See also EMGK.

E.M.G.K. Despite the 1909 regulations, which allocated 'E.M.G.' to the supplementary machine-gun companies (Ersatz-Maschinengewehr-Kompagnien), most of the observed marks included an additional K for 'Kompagnie' in defiance of the rules. They should be considered as unofficial deviations. See also EMG.

Two of the many substitute pistol designs acquired during the First World War. **Top:** *the 7.65mm ACP Dreyse, made by Rheinische Metallwaren- & Maschinenfabrik of Sömmerda from 1907-8 onwards and widely used prewar as a police weapon.* **Above:** *the FL-Selbstlader, by Fritz Langenhahn of Suhl, developed during the early stages of the First World War. (Joe Schroeder.)*

MARKS FA-FTA

F.A. The appearance of these code letters on a weapon usually indicates that it had been issued to one of the Flieger-Abteilungen (airmen's units). Both letters are struck in roman type and the marks read 'F.A.1.15.', for Flieger-Abteilung Nr. 1.

F.A. The presence of these letters indicated that the article on which they appeared had been issued to a Fernsprech-Abteilung (field telephone unit), provided the F was in script. Typical marks read 'F.A.III.35.', the field telephone unit of III.Armeekorps.

F.A.G. These distinguished another of the relatively minor German army units — the Fernsprech-Abteilung des Gardekorps (field telephone unit attached to the Guard Corps). The letter F is struck in script.

F.E.A. This was the mark of a Flieger-Ersatz-Abteilung (supplementary airmen's unit), stamped in the form of 'F.E.A.2.25.'; it is rarely seen on a Pistole 08, however.

F.G. These code letters, sometimes wrongly associated with the Feldgendarmerie or military police, were allocated to the Festungs-Gouvernement by the 1909 marking regulations. A typical mark applied by this organisation, responsible for the upkeep and administration of fortresses and fortifications, reads 'F.G.235.'.

F.M. This mark, applied under the provisions of 1909 regulations, signified one of the less important German army units — a (Feld-)Haubitz-Munitionskolonne, an ammunition column carrying supplies for field howitzers. A typical example reads 'F.M.VII.5.10.' for the 10th weapon issued to the 5th column attached to VII. Armeekorps, but such stampings are rarely found.

F.T.A. This, in which the letters F and T both appeared in script, was the distinguishing mark of the Funken-Telegraphen-Abteilungen (radio-telegraph units), struck as 'F.T.A.1.15.'.

MARKS G-GRU

G. This letter, accompanied by a solitary number, was allocated to the Generalkommando des Gardekorps (corps command section) by the 1909 marking regulations. It was applied simply as 'G.105.'.

G. This was granted to the five Garde-Regimenter zu Fuss (foot guards) in 1909, replacing the 1877-vintage GR mark, and may sometimes be found on handguns. It usually appears in the form '1.G.10.25.', though a few non-standard variations are known.

G.A. These letters identified equipment used by the German Garde-Feldartillerie regiments, four of which existed in August 1914. Generally to be found on the front grip straps of the Reichsrevolvers or Parabellums, The marks often took the form '1.G.A.4.25.'.

G.A.B. This combination of letters was unique to the command units of the Garde-Feldartillerie-Brigade, and was generally applied as 'G.A.B.35.'.

G.A.F. Equipment used by the Garde-Fussartillerie, the foot artillerymen, was marked in this way — '1.G.A.F.1.25.' representing the first battery of a Garde-Fussartillerie-Regiment.

G.A.r. These letters signified a reitende Batterie of the Garde-Feldartillerie-Regiment, appearing on Parabellums and other weapons in the form of '1.G.A.r.2.25.' — the 25th weapon issued to the 2nd mounted battery of 1. Garde Feldartillerie-Regiment.

G.D. The Garde-Dragoner-Regimenter (guard dragoons), two of which existed at the outbreak of the First World War, applied property marks in the form '1.G.D.2.25.'.

G.d.C. The Prussian Regiment des Gardes du Corps, the premier German cavalry regiment, applied unit marks of this type. Pistols were carried prior to 1914, but no wartime product has yet been reported with the stamps — which took the form 'G.d.C.1.25.'.

G.E. These code letters signified the Ersatz-Bataillon of the Garde-Regimenter zu Fuss, or foot guards. A typical specimen reads '1.G.E.4.25.', the 25th weapon issued to the 4th company of the supplementary battalion of 1.Garde-Regiment zu Fuss. See also G.

G.F. This mark distinguished the single Garde-Füsilier-Regiment from ordinary infantry, grenadier or fusilier units, and was granted in 1909 to replace GFR (dating from 1877). It was used in the form 'G.F.10.25.'. Holsters may also bear the letters, especially those made prior to 1914.

G.F.M.G. This combination of code letters represents the machine-gun company (Maschinengewehr-Kompagnie) of the Garde-Füsilier-Regiment, applied under the provisions of the 1909 regulations in the form 'G.F.M.G.35.'. The total of machine-gun companies was increased to two and finally three during the First World War, which means that marks reading 'G.F.3.M.G.35.' may also exist.

G.F.R. This mark was used by the Garde-Füsilier Regiment from 1877 until replaced in 1909 by GF (qv). It is unlikely that GFR will ever be found on a Parabellum apart, perhaps, from a specimen displaying a non-standard mark applied during the First World War.

G.G. This mark was allocated to the five Garde-Grenadier regiments in 1909, replacing GGR (in use since 1877). It may occasionally be found on the grip-straps of Parabellums in the form of '1.G.G.10.25.', and also on the holsters.

G.G.M.G. This series of code letters may be found in unit marks applied by the Maschinengewehr-Kompagnien (machine-gun companies) attached to the Garde-Grenadier-Regimenter, five of which existed prior to 1918. A typical mark reads '2.G.G.M.G.35.' for the 35th weapon issued to the machine-gun company of Garde-Grenadier-Regiment Nr.2, through extra companies (up to three) were added during the First World War and it is possible to find marks reading '2.G.G.2.M.G.35.'.

G.G.R. These property mark-letters were used by the Garde-Grenadier-Regiment from 1877 until replaced by GR in 1909. They will not be found on a Pistole 08, apart from a few stamped unofficially during the First World War.

G.H. This mark was unique to the solitary Leib-Garde-Husaren-Regiment and was applied as 'G.H.3.25.' to handguns, holsters and accessories.

G.İ.B. This letter combination belonged to the command units of the Garde-Infanterie-Brigaden, a typical mark reading '3.G.İ.B.25.' (the 25th weapon issued to 3.Garde-Infanterie-Brigade). Note the dot above the 'I' to distinguish it from the otherwise similar roman numeral.

G.İ.D. This set of letters was set aside by the 1909 marking regulations for the Garde-Infanterie-Divisionen staffs, a typical specimen reading '2.G.İ.D.25.' for the 25th weapon issued to the 2nd guard infantry division. See also GIB.

G.J. These code letters were applied under the 1877 and 1909 marking regulations to weapons used by the Prussian Garde-Jäger-Bataillon (riflemen). They usually appear in the form of 'G.J.3.25.'.

G.J.M.G. This unit marking was applied by the Maschinengewehr-Kompagnie of the Garde-Jäger-Bataillon, taking the form 'G.J.M.G.35.'. It may occasionally be found on the front grip-strap of pre-1918 Pistolen 08 and their holsters.

G.K. This mark was used by the single Prussian Garde-Kürassier-Regiment (guard cuirassiers, heavy cavalry) from 1877 until the end of the First World War, and may be encountered on a handgun or its holster in the form 'G.K.3.25.'.

G.K.B. These letters were reserved for the command units of the Garde-Kavallerie-Brigaden. A typical mark reads '1.G.K.B.135.' for the 135th weapon issued to the 1st guard cavalry brigade.

G.K.D. This marking was used, under the terms of the 1909 regulations, by the Garde-Kavallerie-Division. A typical specimen reads 'G.K.D.75.' for the 75th weapon issued to the staff units of the guard cavalry division, and may sometimes be displayed on a handgun or its holster.

G

Continued
GK-GRU

G.M.G.A. This was applied by the Prussian Garde-Maschinengewehr-Abteilungen, guard machine-gun units, under the terms of the 1909 regulations.

G.P. These code letters were used in markings applied – to Pistolen 08 and other handguns – by the Garde-Pionier-Bataillon, having been introduced by the 1877 regulations. They appear in the form 'G.P.1.55.'.

G.R. (R in script). This mark was applied to the Garde-Reserve-Regimenter – infantrymen – in the form '1.G.R.5.25.'. See also G.

G.R.E. (R in script). This was the mark of the Ersatz or supplementary battalion of a Garde-Reserve-Regiment. It may be found taking the form of '1.G.R.E.4.75.', showing the weapon to have been the 75th issued to the 4th company of the Ersatz-Bataillon der 1.Garde-Reserve-Regiments. See also G and GE.

G.R.Ì.B. (R in script). This mark, applied under the provisions of the 1909 regulations, signified that the weapon on which it appeared had been issued to the command units of a Garde-Reserve-Infanterie-Brigade. A typical sample reads '1.G.R.Ì.B.35.'. See also GIB.

G.R.Ì.D. This property marking was applied by command units of the Garde-Reserve-Infanterie-Divisionen, two of which existed during the First World War. A typical example reads '2.G.R.Ì.D.35.'. See also GID.

G.R.J. (R in script). This mark was applied by units of the Garde-Reserve-Jäger-Bataillon in the form 'G.R.J.1.25.'.

G.R.A. (R in script). This belonged to the Garde-Reserve-Feldartillerie-Regimenter and usually appeared in the form '2.G.R.A.5.25.'. See also GA.

G.R.A.B. (R in script). This marking was used by the command units of the Garde-Reserve-Feldartillerie-Brigade and usually took the form of 'G.R.A.B.25.'. See also GAB.

G.R.D. (R in script). Applied by the Garde-Reserve-Dragoner-Regiment (guard dragoons) prior to 1918, this mark may be encountered in the guise of 'G.R.D.3.25.'. See also GD.

G.R.P. These letters, applied under the provisions of the 1909 marking regulations, signified that the weapon on which they were displayed had been used by the Grenadier-Regiment zu Pferde (mounted grenadiers). Only one such unit existed; numbered in the same sequence as the dragoons, a typical example of its mark reads '3.G.R.P.3.75.' for the 75th weapon issued to the 3rd squadron.

G.R.R. This letter combination was unique to one of the special Saxon cavalry regiments, the Garde-Reiter-Regiment, and was applied as 'G.R.R.2.35.'.

G.R.S. (R in script). This mark was used by the Garde-Reserve-Schützen-Bataillon prior to 1918, in the guise of 'G.R.S.1.25.'. See also GS.

G.R.U. (R in script). These code letters signified that a weapon had been issued to the Garde-Reserve-Ulanen-Regiment, taking the form 'G.R.U.3.75.'. See also GU.

H. This letter-mark belonged to the Husaren-Regimenter (hussars), twenty of which had been raised by the outbreak of the First World War — Prussian: 1-17; Saxon, 18-20. The marks were usually applied as '10.H.2.35.', and may be found on Reichsrevolvers and Parabellums.

H.Q. This set of marks, found in a few pre-1918 German unit stampings, is very desirable — as it shows that the item of equipment on which it appeared had been used by the Grosses Hauptquartier Seiner Majestät des Kaisers, the Kaiser's headquarters. It takes the form 'H.Q.15.', but it must be stressed that no stampings of this pattern have yet been found on a handgun and any that appear may be of questionable authenticity!

İ.B. These code letters were applied, under the terms of the 1909 marking regulations, to the weapons and equipment of the Infanterie-Brigaden (infantry brigades). They were stamped as '5.İ.B.25.', the 25th weapon issued to the command units of the 5th brigade. Note the large dot above the letter 'I', which distinguished it from the similar roman numeral.

İ.D. The presence of these code letters in a property mark signified that the item had been used by an Infanterie-Division. The Germans invariably put a small dot above the letter I, to distinguish it from the roman numeral 'I'. (Note: divisional markings are often found in conjunction with other letters — those of munitions columns and other minor units, for example.)

İ.M. These letters appeared in property marks applied by the Infanterie-Munitionskolonnen (infantry ammunition-supply units) under the 1909 marking regulations. A typical specimen reads 'İ.M.VI.3.25.', for the 25th weapon issued to 3.Infanterie-Munitionskolonne attached to VI. Armeekorps.

MARKS J-JR

J. This letter was applied to weapons issued to the German Jäger-Bataillone (riflemen) from 1877 onwards, as it survived the 1909 reforms unaltered. It appeared in the form '5.J.2.35.' on handguns issued to the following: *Prussian units* — 1-11, 14; *Saxon units* — 12 and 13. There were also two independently-numbered Bavarian rifle battalions, the marks of which, however, were usually prefixed with the letter B. (Note: despite the official insistence of the use of 'J' for 'Jäger', various unofficial marks — notably 'J.B.' — were used during the First World War, when the 'J.' mark was often confusingly used for the 'I.' associated with the infantry, fusilier and grenadier regiments.)

J.E. These code letters appeared in property marks applied by the Ersatz-Abteilungen, or supplementary detachments, of the pre-1918 German Jäger-Bataillone. They were stamped as '5.J.E.2.25.' for the 25th weapon issued to the 2nd company of the supplementary detachment of Jäger-Bataillon Nr. 5.

J.M.G. This mark signified a Jäger battalion's Maschinengewehrkompagnie (machine-gun company); it may occasionally be encountered on handguns in the form '5.J.M.G.25.'. See also J.

J.P. These letters denoted equipment — including pistols — issued to the Prussian mounted riflemen, the Jäger zu Pferde, thirteen regiments of which had been raised by the outbreak of the First World War. The marks take the form of '5.J.P.3.25.'.

J.R. this mark According to the 1909 regulations, was struck on equipment used by the recruiting depot (Rekrutendepot) of a Jäger-Bataillon; '5.J.R.45.', therefore, would be the 45th weapon held on the inventory of the depot of the 5th rifle battalion. Such marks, however, are rarely found.

Directory **6**

 MARKS K-KS

K. The solitary Saxon Karabiner-Regiment is believed to have applied marks in the form of 'K.2.25.', the absence of a prefix number serving to distinguish between it and the Prussian cuirassiers — whose letter-mark was also K.

K. The property marks applied by the Prussian cuirassier units (Kürassier-Regimenter) took the form of '5.K.3.25.'; eight regiments had been raised by the beginning of the First World War.

K.D. The presence of these code letters in a unit marking generally indicates that the weapon or item of equipment was issued to the staff of a cavalry division (Kavallerie-Division). (Note: divisional markings are often found in conjunction with other letters — those of munitions columns and other minor units, for example.)

K.D. The existence of this mark has been reported on naval stores, without much authentication at the time of writing. It allegedly represents 'Kriegsmarine Division' (navy detachment).

K.S. This mark was applied by units of the German colonial forces, the Kaiserliche Schutztruppen, other than those stationed in East Africa, South-West Africa or the Cameroons (see SchDOA, SchDSWA and SchK). The marks probably appear as 'K.S.225.'; none has yet been reported on a pre-1918 Parabellum, but there is no reason to assume that none existed.

Above: *the 1906-pattern Parabellum, distinguished by its grip safety but otherwise much the same as the Pistole 08, was used by officers as a privatwaffe — or non-issue weapon (Rolf Gminder).*

Above: *the DWM-made 1908-type Parabellum pistol was supplied in small quantities to the Bulgarian army just prior to the beginning of the First World War. The guns had lanyard rings on the butt-heels and lion marks on the toggles and receivers (Rolf Gminder).*

Directory **7**

MARKS L–LR

L. This code letter was used on handguns issued to the Bavarian Leib-Infanterie-Regiment, though it usually appeared as 'B.L.5.45.' rather than simply 'L.5.45.'.

L.A. These marks were applied by the Feldluftschiffer-Abteilungen, the field airship detachments, and may be found as 'L.A.1.15.', the 15th weapon issued to Abteilung Nr. 1. They are rarely seen on handguns, however.

L.A.E. Applied under the provisions of the 1909 handbook, this mark belonged to the Luftschiffer-Ersatz-Abteilung, or supplementary airship (or balloon) detachment. It appears as 'L.A.E.2.15.', for the 15th weapon issued to the 2nd company. See also LA.

L.A.R. According to the 1909 regulations, this mark was used by the recruiting depot of the supplementary airship (or balloon) detachment — the Rekrutendepot der Luft-schiffer-Ersatz-Abteilung.

l.F.M. (to be read as 'L.F.M.'). These letters were applied by the leichte Feldhaubitz-Munitionskolonnen, munitions columns carrying ammunition for the light field howitzers. They were usually applied as '1.F.M.II.52.10.' — the remainder of the stamp indicating that the column was attached to II. Abteilung of Feldartillerie-Regiment Nr. 52 — but are rarely if ever found on Pistolen 08. Revolvers and other second-rate handguns were normally carried.

l.H.M. (to be read as 'L.H.M.'). These appeared in the property stamps applied by a leichte (Feld-)Haubitz-Munitionskolonne — an ammunition column carrying shells, etc., for light field howitzers. See also 'l.F.M.' for details of the marks themselves; they are, however, rarely found on handguns.

L.L. These code letters, introduced by a December 1910 amendment to the 1909 regulations (to replace ML — qv), distinguished the equipment of the Feldtrupp für Lenkluftschiffe and were applied in the form 'L.L.1.15.'. The field dirigible detachment was disbanded in 1917, when its airships were transferred to the naval section.

L.L.E. This German unit mark was applied, in the form of 'L.L.E.55.', by the Ersatztruppe für Lenkluftschiffe from December 1910 until 1917. It has yet to be found on a pistol; see also LL.

l.M. (to be read as 'L.M.'). These letters distinguished another minor German army unit, a leichte Munitions-kolonne, or light ammunition supply column. If the mark simply reads 'l.M.II.5.25.', then the weapon was issued to the column attached to II. Abteilung of the 5th field artillery regiment; but see also lMAF.

L.M.G. This mark was introduced by a November 1909 amendment to the original 1909 marking handbook, for the Lehr-Maschinengewehr-Kompagnie der Infanter-Schiess-Schule — the machine-gun training company attached to the infantry marksmanship school at Spandau. Taking the form of 'L.M.G.55.', it has been reported on a Pistole 08.

l.M...K.D. This mark, to be read as 'L.M.K.D.', was applied by the leichte Munitionskolonnen attached to the Kavallerie-Divisionen — light ammunition supply columns attached to cavalry divisions. A typical example reads 'l.M.2.K.D.25.' for the 25th weapon issued to the light supply column accompanying the 2nd such cavalry unit.

l.M...R. (R in script). This combination of letters appeared in property markings applied by one of the less important pre-1918 army units — a light ammunition supply column, or leichte Munitionskolonne, attached to a reserve field artillery regiment. A typical example may read 'l.M.II.5.R.50.', for the 50th weapon issued to the light column attached to II.Abteilung of the 5th reserve field artillery regiment.

l.M.r. This combination of letters may be found in the property marks applied by some obscure German army units, the light ammunition supply columns attached to mounted detachments of the field artillery regiments (leichte Munitionskolonnen der reitende Abteilungen des Feldartillerie-Regimenter). A typical example reads 'l.M.r.5.25.' for the 25th weapon issued to the supply column of the 5th field artillery regiment's mounted detachment, but marks of this pattern are rarely seen.

L.R. This property marking belonged to the Lehr-Infanterie-Bataillon, a relatively insignificant training unit, and usually appeared in the guise of 'L.R.5.105.' — the 105th weapon issued to the 5th company.

MARKS M–ML

M.A. These letters are believed to have been the abbreviation of Matrosen-Artillerie-Abteilung, five of which were formed during the Second Reich. The marks of these coast artillery units would, therefore, read 'IV.M.A.51.'.

M.A. This naval abbreviation, signifying Minenabteilung (minelaying and minesweeping detachment), has yet to be found on a German naval Parabellum. However, small numbers of artillery Parabellums — the langen Pistolen 08 — are said to have been reissued to personnel of gunboats and inshore minesweepers towards the end of the First World War, and some may even have been specially marked. The stamps are assumed to have read 'M.A.51.' or, perhaps, 'I.M.A.51.' even though there was only a single detachment.

M.D. These letters may occasionally be found on the grip straps of naval Parabellums, the Pistolen 04. They signify Matrosen-Division (sailors division), two of which existed in 1914, and take the form of 'II.M.D.51.'; all non-technical seagoing personnel belonged to one of these units.

M.G.A. This mark was used by the independent machine-gun detachments (Maschinengewehr-Abteilungen), 19 of which had been formed by August 1914. The stamps were usually applied as '3.M.G.A.25.' but some non-standard variations have been seen.

M.G.A.E. This mark was used by the Ersatz-Maschinengewehr-Abteilungen, either as 'M.G.A.E.25.' or 'l.M.G.A.E.25.'.

M.L. This short-lived unit marking, introduced by the 1909 regulations for the Motorluftschiffer-Abteilungen (powered airship detachments) and applied as 'M.L.1.25.' for the first such unit, was superseded in December 1910 by LL (qv). It has not been found on a pistol at the time of writing.

O. This letter, when used in the form 'O.VI.45.', signified a weapon used by the high command of an army — in this case, the 6th. Few marks of this type have yet been found.

O.E. Dating from the early 1900s, this signifies 'Ostasiatisches Expeditionskorps', a German military force despatched to China at the time of the Boxer Rebellion. It has occasionally been linked with the Parabellum (in particular, with the 1900 pattern), but its existence on any of the guns acquired by the German army for trials has never been confirmed. A typical mark would read 'O.E.45.'. See also OR.

O.R. This abbreviation is associated with the German Ostasiatisches Infanterie-Regimenter, raised to serve in the Far East in the early 1900s. Though marks in the form '1.O.R.2.45.' have been found on Gewehre 98, none has yet been seen on a handgun. See also OE.

P. This letter-mark was applied to the equipment of the Pionier-Bataillone (pioneers), thirty of which were in existence in August 1914 — *Prussian:* 1-11, 14-21 and 23-30; *Saxon:* 12 and 22; *Wurttembergian:* 13. The stamp took the form '15.P.3.25.', but is only occasionally encountered on Parabellums.

 MARKS R-RU

R. This letter signified any of the German infantry, fusilier or grenadier regiments, coming into use in 1877 and surviving unchanged through the reforms of 1909. It was used in the form '27.R.10.25.' by the following units: *Prussian infantry* — 13-32, 41-72, 74-9, 81-5, 87-8, 91-9, 111-32, 135-8 and 140-76; *Prussian fusiliers* — 33-40, 73, 80, 86 and 90; and *Prussian grenadiers* — 1-12, 89, 109-10; *Saxon infantry* — 102-7, 133-4, 139, 177-9 and 181-2; *Saxon fusiliers* — 108; and *Saxon grenadiers* — 100-1; and *Wurttemberg regiments* — 119-27 and 180. Bavarian infantry units, numbered in a separate sequence, usually had their marks preceded by the letter B.

R. This letter, when it appeared by itself in script (as '25.R.3.25.'), signified a Reserve-Infanterie-Regiment — assuming that it had been applied under the 1909 regulations, when it had replaced the 1877-vintage mark of one roman and one script R. A single cursive R had been used by the Reiter-Regimenter, cavalry units, in the 1877-1909 period.

R.A. (R in script). These marks were applied — in the form of '10.R.A.2.25.' — by the German army's Reserve-Feldartillerie-Regimenter. See also A.

R.A.F. (R in script). This combination of letters was used by the Reserve-Fussartillerie-Regimenter prior to 1918, applied to equipment as '5.R.A.F.2.25.'. See also AF.

R.A.F.M. or R.A.F...M. (R in script). These marks often appear — though rarely on Pistolen 08 — in the form '2.R.A.F.II.1.M.25.', which would indicate 1.Munitionskolonne attached to II-Bataillon of 2.Reserve-Fussartillerie-Regiment: the 1st ammunition column attached to the 2nd battalion of the reserve foot artillery regiment.

R.A.M. (R in script). This was the mark of a Reserve-Artillerie-Munitionskolonne, applied under the provisions of the 1909 regulations. This type of insignificant unit rarely carried Pistolen 08 — especially during the First World War, when Parabellums were needed in the front line — but at least one, a 1912-vintage Erfurt specimen, has been reported with the marks of Reserve-Artillerie-Munitionskolonne Nr.4 on its grip-strap. See also AM.

R.D. (R in script). These markings were applied by the Reserve-Dragoner-Regimenter under the regulations of 1877 and 1909. A typical example reads '5.R.D.2.75.'.

M 04 naval and P 08 army Parabellums

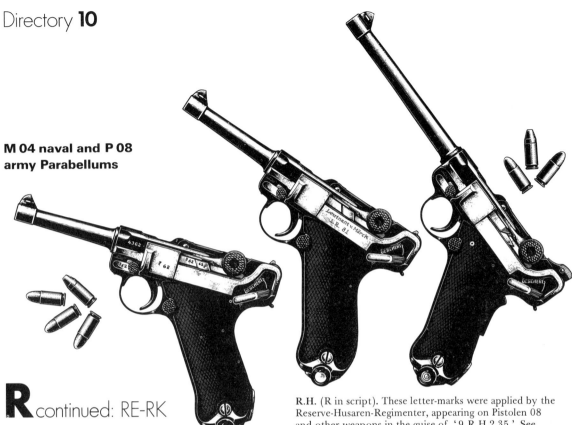

R continued: RE-RK

R.E. This mark was applied under the marking regulations of 1877 and 1909 to equipment used by the Ersatz-Bataillone of the standard infantry regiments. Consequently, '15.R.E.2.25.' was the 25th weapon issued to the 2nd company of the 'Ersatz' or supplementary battalion of the 15th infantry regiment.

R.E. (R in script). This mark was applied by the Ersatz-Bataillone of the reserve infantry regiments under the 1909 regulations. See also RE.

R.E.D. This was applied, under the provisions of the 1909 regulations, to a relatively obscure infantry unit — an Ersatz-depot of a regiment. It is found as '15.R.E.D. 55.', but rarely on a handgun.

R.E.D. (R in script). This mark was applied, in the form of '15.R.E.D.55.', to the Ersatz-depot of a reserve infantry regiment. See also RED.

R.E.E. (R in script). This obscure army unit marking was used by the Reserve-Ersatz-Eskadron of an army corps, taking the form 'R.E.E.XVI.25' — the 25th weapon issued to the reserve supplementary squadron, a cavalry unit, of the 16th army corps. Stampings of this pattern have yet to be reported on pistols.

R.H. (R in script). These letter-marks were applied by the Reserve-Husaren-Regimenter, appearing on Pistolen 08 and other weapons in the guise of '9.R.H.2.35.'. See also H.

R.I.B. (R in script). This mark was applied, in accordance with the 1909 regulations, by command units of a Reserve-Infanterie-Brigade. A typical specimen reads '5.R.I.B.25.'. See also IB.

R.I.D. (R in script). This, applied as '3.R.I.D.25.', was associated with the command units of — in this case — 3.Reserve-Infanterie-Division. See also ID.

R.I.M. (R in script). This combination of letters signified that the weapon on which they appeared had been issued to one of the Reserve-Infanterie-Munitionskolonnen. A typical example reads 'R.I.M.4.35.'. See also IM.

R.J. (R in script). This mark was used by the Reserve-Jäger-Bataillone prior to 1918, the marks appearing as '5.R.J.3.25.'. See also J.

R.J.P. (R in script). This pre-1918 property mark was unique to the solitary Reserve-Jäger-Regiment zu Pferde and appeared as 'R.J.P.3.45.'. It may, perhaps, be found on the occasional handgun. See also JP.

R.K. (R in script). This was associated with the Bavarian Reserve-Kavallerie-Regimenter, three of which had been raised by 1918. See BRK.

R.M.G. These letters, introduced by an amendment to the 1909 regulations issued in April 1911, identified the equipment of the machine-gun companies (Maschinen-gewehr-Kompagnien) of the infantry regiments, being applied as '25.R.M.G.35.'. During the First World War the machine-gun strength of some regiments was raised from one company to three, in which cases the marks could read '25.R.2.M.G.35.' for a sidearm issued to the second machine-gun unit.

R.M.G. (R in script). This particular combination of code letters belonged to some short-lived units, the Reserve-Maschinengewehr-Kompagnien or reserve machine-gun companies. The mark was introduced by an amendment to the 1909 regulations issued in May 1910 and deleted in April 1911. It took the form of 'R.M.G.1.25.' for the 1st reserve company.

R.M.G.K. During 1917, the Germans issued light machine-guns to each company of the infantry regiments, providing in effect, a company machine-gun troop. Several pistols have been seen with the distinctive markings of these, which were supposed to read '25.R.M.G.5.K.35.' for a weapon issued to the Maschinengewehrtrupp of the 5th company of Infanterie-Regiment Nr. 25. However, a variety of non-standard and unofficial stampings has been reported.

R.R. (both letters in roman type). This set of letter-punches was applied, under the 1909 regulations, by the Rekrutendepot (recruiting depot) of an infantry regiment. The marks take the form of '25.R.R.35.' but are rarely if ever found.

R.R. (one script letter, one roman letter). This mark signified the recruiting depot of a reserve infantry regi-ment, if applied under the 1909 regulations; or a reserve infantry regiment itself under the earlier 1877 code. The former is rarely if ever found on a Parabellum; the latter, never.

R.U. (R in script). This combination of code letters appeared on weapons and equipment issued to the Reserve-Ulanen-Regimenter in the form '5.R.U.3.45.'. There were seven such units by the time of the First World War, all except one of which were Prussian. The other was Saxon. See also U.

MARKS S-StSB

S.A. This code-mark was unique, so far as the pre-1918 German army was concerned, to the independent signal detachments (the Feldsignal-Abteilungen) and was used as 'S.A.2.25.' for the 25th weapon of the 2nd unit. Stamp-ings of this type have been reported on Parabellums of the 1909-18 era, though the authenticity of many is question-able; similar marks are said to have been applied to the weapons of the Sturm-Abteilungen during the Third Reich.

S.A.E. This mark, applied under the 1909 regulations, belonged to the Ersatz-Signal-Abteilungen or supplemen-tary signal detachments. It was used as 'S.A.E.5.25.', for the 25th weapon issued to the 5th detachment. See also SA.

S.B. This property mark was applied by the three German Seebataillone or marines, and is sometimes encountered on naval Parabellums in the form 'II.S.B.51.'. The third 'sea battalion' was stationed in the Far East, at Tsingtao.

Sch.D.O.A. This unit mark was applied by the German colonial forces in East Africa, the Schutztruppe für Deutsch-Ostafrika, prior to 1918. It invariably appeared as 'Sch.D.O.A.715.'. The units were based in Dar-es-Salaam.

s.R. (R in script). This mark was confined to the Prussian schweres Reserve-Reiter-Regimenter, or heavy reserve cavalry units — three of which existed in 1918. The marks took the form of '2.s.R.5.75.' and may occasionally be encountered, but it should be noted that there were two Bavarian heavy cavalry regiments that applied the same sR (script R) stampings even though they were line rather than reserve units; however, their marks were usually pre-fixed by an additional letter B. There was no Prussian line heavy cavalry.

s.R. This mark was associated with the Bavarian schweres Reiter-Regimenter — heavy cavalrymen — but was more normally written as 'B.s.R.' (qv).

St.S.B. This abbreviation, not yet identified on a naval Parabellum, is believed to have been applied by 3.Stamm-seebataillon — the depot unit of 3.Seebataillon, which was on far eastern service at Tsingtao. The depot lay in Cuxhaven.

Directory **11**

MARKS T–TS

T. There were 21 Train-Abteilungen in existence at the beginning of the First World War (prior to March 1914 they had been called 'Train Bataillone') — *Prussian*: 1-11, 14-18, 20 and 21; *Saxon*: 12, 19; *Wurttembergian*: 13. Their property marks took the form of '15.T.2.25.', though these are only occasionally found on Parabellums as the Train often carried the old revolvers and other second-rate handguns.

T. (script). This letter signified Telegraph or Telegraphen-truppen, but in such cases rarely appeared by itself — see ATA and TAG. If took the form *𝒯* in Prussia, Saxony and Württemberg , but was written as *𝒞* in Bavaria; however, it is not usually found on Parabellums, as the telegraph units were armed with revolvers or second-rate pistols.

T.A.G. This, when found in a unit marking, represented the Telegraphen-Abteilung des Garde-Korps (telegraph unit of the guard corps) and appeared as 'T.A.G.25.' with the T in script.

T.B. Appearing as '9.T.B.2.25.', this was the mark of a Feld-Bäckerei-Kolonne, or field bakery unit, formed from a Train-Abteilung (in this case, the 9th).

T.D. These letters were an abbreviated form of Torpedo-Division, a German naval unit, and may be found on the grip straps of Pistolen 04 — taking the form 'I.T.D.51.'. Two such detachments existed at the outbreak of the First World War.

T.E. This mark was used by the Ersatz-Abteilungen of the Train-Abteilungen, as '5.T.E.2.25.' for the 25th weapon issued to the 2nd squadron of the supplementary battalion of the 5th train detachment. Units of this type, however, rarely carried Parabellums as the older revolvers or other second-rate handguns were used instead.

T.F. This abbreviation signified a Fuhrparkkolonne or transport park unit, formed by a Train-Abteilung. See also TB.

T.L. These letters were applied by a Feldlazarett or field hospital, formed from a Train-Abteilung; the marks usually read '9.T.L.3.23.'. See also TB.

T.P. This stamp was used by a Proviant-Kolonne, or supply column, formed from a Train-Abteilung and usually read '9.T.P.3.25.'. See also TB.

T.P.D. This abbreviation was used by a Pferde-Depot, or horse depot, formed from a Train-Abteilung. A typical example read '9.T.P.D.3.25.'. See also TB.

T.S. These letters were applied by the Sanitäts-Kompagn-ien (sanitary detachments) formed from Train-Abteilungen and usually read '9.T.S.1.25.'. See also TB.

MARKS U–WW

U. This code letter was used in property marks applied by the many Ulanen-Regimenter (lancers) that existed in August 1914 — *Prussian*: 1-16; *Saxon*: 17, 18 and 21; *Wurttembergian*: 19 and 20. The stampings usually read '5.U.3.25.' and may often be found on the grip straps of Pistolen 08, as well as on the holsters and other articles.

U.A. This would signify a weapon used by the Unter-seeboot-Abteilung (submarine detachment) during the pre-1918 period. It has not yet been found on an example of the Pistole 04, on which the mark would probably take the form of 'U.A.51.' or possibly 'I.U.A.51.'; there was, however, only a single submarine detachment.

W.D. This was the mark of a Werft-Division or dockyard unit and may occasionally be found on naval equipment, including some Pistolen 04 (Parabellums) that display it on the grip-strap. All technical personnel belonged to one of the two Werft-Divisionen, while all other sailors, sea-going or otherwise, were a part of the Matrosen-Divisionen (see MD). (Note: the WD mark of a Werft-Division can be confused with the similar abbreviation used by the 'Werft Danzig' or Danzig dockyard, the former was written as 'II.W.D.51.' and the latter simply as 'W.D.51.' without a roman numeral prefix.)

W.D. Pre-1918 1904-pattern naval Parabellums may occasionally be encountered with these letters stamped into the grip strap, showing that they were held on the inventory of Werft Danzig — Danzig dockyard.

W.K. This mark was used on Parabellums — naval Pistolen 04 — belonging to the Werft Kiel, Kiel dockyard.

W.W. The Wilhelmshaven dockyard (Werft Wilhelmshaven) applied marks of this type to its equipment and weaponry. A few naval 1904-pattern Parabellums have been seen with them, invariably on the grip-strap.

Directory **12**

PART SEVEN

The issue of pistols in 1914

Many soldiers carried Parabellums or, notably during the early part of the First World War, the older revolvers. Most men also carried edged weapons, details of which are also given. To prevent needless repetition, abbreviations have been used — *a/A*, alter Art or old pattern. *AOS*, Artillerie-Offizier-Säbel. *AS*, Artillerie-Säbel. *GROD*, Garde-Reiter-Offizier-Degen (Saxony only). *GRS*, Garde-Reiter-Säbel (Saxony only). *IOD*, Infanterie-Offizier-Degen. *IOS*, Infanterie-Offizier-Säbel (Bavaria and Saxony only). *IS 38*, Infanterie-Säbel Model 1838 (Bavaria only). *KOS*, Kavallerie-Offizier-Säbel, *KS*, Kavallerie-Säbel. *KS 98* Kurzes Seitengewehr Modell 1898. *OP*, Offizier-Pallasch (Bavaria only). *P*, Pallasch (Bavaria only). *S 71 S.* Seitengewehr Modell 1871 'mit Sägerücken' (saw-backed). *S 71/84*, Seitengewehr Modell 1898. *S 98/05 S.* Seitengewehr Modell 1898/05 'mit Sägerücken'. *SfF*, Seitengewehr für Fahnenträger. *S u/M*, Seitengewehr umgeändertes Muster. *TOS*, Train-Offizier-Säbel (Saxony only). *TS*, Train-Säbel.

Glossary of key terms and ranks

Berittene: mounted. *Bespannungs:* horse-drawn. *Einjahrig-Freiwilligen:* volunteer serving for one year. *Fahnenträger:* standard bearer. *Fahrer:* driver. *Feldwebel:* sergeant-major. *Gefreiter:* lance-corporal. *Gemeine:* 'other ranks'. *Hilfs:* assistant, deputy. *Kapitulant:* trainee non-commissioned officer. *Mannschaften:* 'men'. *Pionier:* sapper. *Radfahrer:* cyclist. *Sanitäts:* medical. *Tambour:* drummer. *Trompeter:* bugler or trumpeter. *Unteroffizier:* corporal. *Vizefeldwebel:* sergeant. *Vizewachtmeister:* cavalry sergeant. *Wachtmeister.* cavalry sergeant-major. *Waffenmeister:* armourer. *Zu Fuss:* on foot, dismounted.

Small numbers of the 7.65mm Parabellum of 1900 (below) and the 9mm 1906 pattern (right) were acquired privately by the German army officers, especially in the period before the adoption of the P 08. Note the toggle-lock (inset) on the earlier pattern. (Rolf Gminder.)

Infantry   Prussia

Garde-Regiment zu Fuss. Armed as infantry (qv). Typical mark: '1.G.10.25.'– 1. Garde-Regiment zu Fuss, 10th company, weapon number 25. Regiments concerned: 1 to 5.

Garde-Grenadier-Regiment. Armed as infantry (qv). Typical mark: '1.G.G.10.25.' – Kaiser Alexander Garde-Grenadier-Regiment Nr. 1, 10th company, weapon number 25. Regiments concerned: 1 to 5.

Grenadier-Regiment. Armed as infantry (qv). Typical mark: '6.R.10.25.' – Grenadier-Regiment Graf Kleist von Nollendorf (1. Westpreussisches) Nr. 6, 10th company, weapon number 25. Regiments concerned: 1 to 12, 89 (Mecklenburg), and 109 and 110 (Baden), numbered in the same sequence as the infantry regiments.

Infanterie-Regiment. Armed as noted. Typical mark: '27.R.10.25.' – Infanterie-Regiment Prinz Louis Ferdinand von Preussen (2. Magdeburgisches) Nr. 27, 10th company, weapon number 25. Regiments concerned: 13 to 32, 41 to 72, 74 to 79, 81 to 85, 87, 88, 91 to 99, 111 to 132, 135 to 138, and 140 to 176.
Feldwebel: P 08 and IOD
Vizefeldwebel: same
Fahnenträger: P 08, and IOD or SfF
Regiments- und Batallion Tambours: P 08, and IOD or S 98
Entfernungsmesser (Hahn): P 08 and S 98
Sanitätsmannschaften: P 08, and S 98 or IOD
Machine-gun companies. Typical mark: '27.R.M.G.25.' – Infanterie-Regiment Prinz Louis Ferdinand von Preussen (2. Magdeburgisches) Nr. 27, machine-gun company, weapon number 25.
Feldwebel: P 08 and IOD
Vizefeldwebel: same
Berittene Unteroffiziere: P 08 and KS
Unteroffiziere: P 08 and S 71/84
Mannschaften: same
Sanitätsmannschaften: P 08, and S 71/84 or IOD
Note: units from Mecklenburg (Grenadier-Regiment Nr. 89) and Hessen (Infanterie-Regimenter Nr. 115-18 and 168) carried distinctive 'state pattern' swords, but were otherwise identically armed with the Prussian troops.

Garde-Füsilier-Regiment. Armed as infantry (qv). Typical mark: 'G.F.10.25.' – 10th company, weapon number 25.

Füsilier-Regiment. Armed as infantry (qv). Typical mark: '36.R.10.25.'– Füsilier-Regiment Generalfeldmarschall Graf Blumenthal (Magdeburgisches) Nr. 36, 10th company, weapon number 25. Regiments concerned: 33 to 40, 73, 80, 86 and 90 (Mecklenburg), in the same sequence as the infantry regiments.

Bavaria

Leib-Infanterie-Regiment. Armed as infantry (qv). Typical mark: 'L.5.45.', or sometimes 'B.L.5.45.'

Infanterie-Regiment. Armed as noted. Typical mark: 'B.16.R.5.45.' – 16. Bayerisches Infanterie-Regiment Grossherzog Ferdinand von Toskana, 5th company, weapon number 45. Regiments concerned: 1 to 23.
Feldwebel: P 08 and IOS
Vizefeldwebel: same
Fahnenträger: P 08, and IOS or SfF
Regiments- und Batallion Tambours: P 08, and IOS or IS 38
Entfernungsmesser (Hahn): P 08 and S 98
Sanitätsmannschaften: P 08, and IS 38 or IOS
Machine-gun companies. Typical mark: 'B.16.R.M.G.45.' – 16. Bayerisches Infanterie-Regiment Grossherzog Ferdinand von Toskana, machine-gun company, weapon number 45.
Feldwebel: P 08 and IOS
Vizefeldwebel: same
Berittene Unteroffiziere: P 08 and KS a/A
Unteroffiziere: P 08 and S 71/84
Mannschaften: same
Sanitätsmannschaften: P 08, and IS 38 or IOS

Saxony

The Saxon infantry was armed in much the same manner as the Prussians, but a distinctive 'state pattern' Infanterie-Offizier-Säbel was substituted for the Prussian Infanterie-Offizier-Degen. Typical mark: as Prussia. Units concerned: 1.(Leib-)Grenadier-Regiment Nr. 100, 2.Grenadier-Regiment Nr. 101, Schützen(Füsilier)-Regiment Nr. 108, Infanterie-Regimenter Nr. 102 to 107, 133, 134, 139, 177 to 179, 181 and 182.

Wurttbg

As Prussia, but with a distinctive 'state pattern' IOD. Regiments concerned: Infanterie-Regimenter Nr 120, 121, 124 to 127 and 180, Grenadier-Regimenter Nr 110 and 123, and Füsilier-Regimenter Nr 122.

Riflemen

Prussia

Garde-Jäger-Bataillon and Garde-Schützen-Bataillon. Armed as Jäger (qv). Typical marks: 'G.J.3.25.', 'G.S.3.25.' — Garde-Jäger-Bataillon and Garde-Schützen-Bataillon, 3rd company, weapon number 25.

Jäger-Bataillon. Armed as noted. Typical mark: '2.J.3.25.' — Jäger-Bataillon Graf Yorck von Wartenburg (Ostpreussisches) Nr. 2, 3rd company, weapon number 25. Units concerned: 1-11, 14 (Mecklenburg). Jäger, Schützen and Radfahrer-Kompagnien:
Feldwebel: P 08 and IOD
Vizefeldwebel: same
Fahnenträger: P 08 and IOD, or SfF
Entfernungsmesser (Hahn): P 08 and S 98
Sanitätsvizefeldwebel: P 08 and IOD
Sanitätsmannschaften: P 08 and S 98
Machine-gun companies. Typical mark: '5.J.M.G.15.' — Jäger-Bataillon von Neumann (1.Schlesisches) Nr. 5, machine-gun company, weapon number 15. Armed as infantry (qv).

Bavaria

The two Bavarian Jäger-Bataillone, numbers 1 and 2, carried the same weapons as the state infantrymen (qv) apart from the Sanitätsmann-schaften, who were issued with the IS 38. Typical mark: 'B.1.J.3.25.'— 1.Bayerisches Jäger-Bataillon König, 3rd company, weapon number 25.

Saxony

The two Saxon Jäger-Bataillone, numbered 12 and 13 in the same sequence as the Prussian units, carried the same weapons as the Prussian Jäger. The Saxon Infanterie-Offizier-Säbel was, however, substituted for the Prussian Infanterie-Offizier-Degen.

Wurttbg

No Jäger troops.

Machine-gunners

Prussia

Garde-Maschinengewehr-Abteilung. Armed as regular units (qv). Typical mark: 'G.M.G.A.1.25.' — Garde-Maschinengewehr-Abteilung Nr. 1, weapon number 25. Units concerned: 1 and 2.

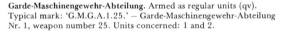

Maschinengewehr-Abteilung. Armed as noted: mark, '3.M.G.A.15.' or 'M.G.A.3.15.' — Maschinengewehr-Abteilung Nr. 3, weapon number 15. Units concerned: 1 to 7.
Feldwebel: P 08 and IOD
Vizefeldwebel: same
Sergeanten: P 08 and AS
Unteroffiziere: same
Trompeter: same
Kapitulanten: same
Fahrer: same
Waffenmeister-Unteroffiziere: P 08, and KOS or IOD
Sanitätsmannschaften: P 08 and AS, or as infantry (qv)

Festungs-Maschinengewehr-Abteilung. Armed as infantry machine-gun companies (qv).

Bavaria

The single Bavarian machine-gun unit, 1.Bayerische Maschinengewehr-Abteilung, was armed as the Bavarian infantry machine-gun companies (qv).

Saxony

The independent Saxon machine-gun unit, number 8 continuing the Prussian sequence, carried much the same weapons as the Prussians, except that the 'state pattern' Infanterie-Offizier-Säbel replaced the Infanterie-Offizier-Degen.

Wurttbg

No comparable units.

Pioneers

Prussia

Garde-Pionier-Bataillon. Armed as regular pioneer battalions (qv). Typical mark: 'G.P.1.55.' — 1st company, weapon number 55.

Pionier-Bataillon. Armed as noted. Typical mark: '3.P.2.25.' — Pionier-Bataillon von Rauch (Brandenburgisches) Nr. 3, 2nd company, weapon number 25. Units concerned: 1-11, 14 to 21, 23 to 30.
Feldwebel: P 08 and IOD
Vizefeldwebel: same
Sanitätsvizefeldwebel: same
Sanitätsmannschaften: P 08 and S 98/05 S
Scheinwerferzüge (additional ranks)
Fahnenschmiede: P 08 and AS
Fahrer: same

Bavaria

The four Bavarian pioneer battalions carried the same weapons as their Prussian counterparts, but an Artillerie-Offizier-Säbel replaced the Infanterie-Offizier-Degen where applicable. Typical mark: 'B.2.P.5.35.' — 2.Bayerisches Pionier-Bataillon, 5th company, weapon number 35.

Saxony

The two Saxon pioneer battalions, 12 and 22, carried the same weapons as the Prussian units, except that the Infanterie-Offizier-Säbel was substituted for the Infanterie-Offizier-Degen. Typical mark: as Prussia.

Wurttbg

Pionier-Bataillon Nr. 13 (Württembergisches) was armed in the same manner as the Prussian and Saxon units, but carried a distinctive 'state pattern' Infanterie-Offizier-Degen. Typical mark: as Prussia.

Cavalry

Prussia

Regiment der Gardes du Corps. Armed as cuirassiers (qv). Typical mark: 'G.d.D.2.25.', the 25th weapon issued to the end squadron.

Garde-Dragoner-Regiment. Armed as dragoons (qv). Typical mark: '1.G.D.3.35.' — 1.Garde-Dragoner-Regiment Königin Viktoria von Grossbritannien und Irland, 3rd squadron, weapon number 35. Regiments concerned: 1 and 2.

Dragoner-Regiment. Armed as noted. Typical mark: '3.D.3.25.' — Grenadier-Regiment zu Pferde Freiherr von Derfflinger (Neumärk-isches) Nr. 3, 3rd squadron, weapon number 25. (This, despite its title, was a dragoon regiment.) Regiments concerned: 1 to 24.
Wachtmeister: P 08 and KOS
Vizewachtmeister: same
Fähnriche: P 08 and KD
Trompeter: same
Hilfstrompeter: same
Sergeanten: P 08, KD, lance
Unteroffiziere: same
Sanitätsmannschaften: P 08, and KOS or KD

Leib-Garde-Husaren-Regiment. Armed as dragoons (qv). Typical mark: 'G.H.3.25.' — 3rd squadron, weapon number 25.

Husaren-Regiment. Armed as dragoons (qv). Typical mark: '5.H.2.25.' — Husaren-Regiment Fürst Blücher von Wahlstatt (Pommersches) Nr. 5, 3rd squadron, weapon number 25. Regiments concerned: 1 to 17.

Garde-Ulanen-Regiment. Armed as dragoons (qv). Typical mark: '2.G.U.2.20.' — 2.Garde-Ulanen-Regiment, 2nd squadron, weapon number 20. Regiments concerned: 1 to 3.

Ulanen-Regiment. Armed as dragoons (qv). Typical mark: '11.U.2.20.' — Ulanen-Regiment Graf Haeseler (2. Brandenburgisches) Nr. 11, 2nd squadron, weapon number 20. Regiments concerned: 1 to 16.

Jäger zu Pferde. Armed as noted. Typical mark: '1.J.P.3.25.' — Regiment Königs-Jäger zu Pferde Nr. 1, 3rd squadron, weapon number 25. Regiments concerned: 1 to 13.
Wachtmeister: P 08 and KürOD
Vizewachtmeister: same
Fähnriche: P 08 and KD
Trompeter: same
Hilfstrompeter: same
Sergeanten: P 08, KD and lance
Unteroffiziere: same
Sanitätsmannschaften: P 08, and KürOD or KD

Garde-Kürassier-Regiment. Armed as cuirassiers (qv). Typical mark: 'G.K.3.35.' — 3rd squadron, weapon number 35.

Kürassier-Regiment. Armed as noted. Typical mark: '5.K.3.35.' — Kürassier-Regiment Herzog Friedrich Eugen von Württemberg (Westpreussisches) Nr. 5, 3rd squadron, weapon number 35. Regiments concerned: 1 (Leib), 2 to 8.
Wachtmeister: P 08 and KürOD
Vizewachtmeister: same
Fähnriche: P 08 and KürD
Trompeter: same
Hilfstrompeter: same
Sergeanten: P 08, KürD and lance
Unteroffiziere: same
Sanitätsmannschaften: P 08, and KürOD or KürD

Note: Prussian units raised in Baden, Braunschweig, Hessen, Mecklenburg, and Oldenburg carried 'state pattern' swords and sabres. These were Dragoner-Regimenter Nr 17 to Nr 24 (17 and 18 Mecklenburg, 19 Oldenburg, 20-22 Baden, and 23 and 24 Hessen) and Husaren-Regiment Nr 17, raised in Braunschweig.

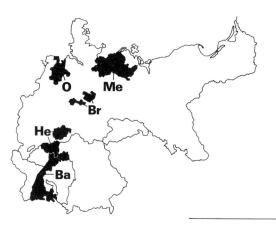

Bavaria

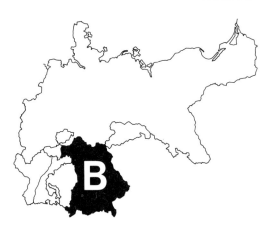

Schweres Reiter-Regiment. Armed as noted. Typical mark: '1.s.ℛ.2.25.' — 1.Schweres Reiter-Regiment Prinz Karl von Bayern, 2nd squadron, weapon number 25. Regiments concerned: 1 and 2.
Wachtmeister: P 08 and OP
Vizewachtmeister: same
Fähnriche: P 08 and P
Trompeter: same
Hilfstrompeter: same
Sergeanten: P 08, P and lance
Unteroffiziere: same
Sanitätsmannschaften: P 08, and OP or P

Ulanen-Regiment. Armed as noted. Typical mark: 'B.1.U.3.25.' — 1.Bayerisches Ulanen-Regiment Kaiser Wilhelm II, König von Preussen, 3rd squadron, weapon number 25. Regiments concerned: 1 and 2.
Wachtmeister: P 08 and KOS
Vizewachtmeister: same
Fähnriche: P 08 and KS 91
Trompeter: same
Hilfstrompeter: same
Sergeanten: P 08, KS 91 and lance
Unteroffiziere: same
Sanitätsmannschaften: P 08, and KOS or KS 91

Chevaulegers-Regiment. Armed as Ulanen (qv). Typical mark: '3.Ch.3.25.' or 'B.3.Ch.3.25.' — 3.Chevaulegers-Regiment Herzog Karl Theodor, 2nd squadron, weapon number 25. Regiments concerned: 1 to 8.

Saxony

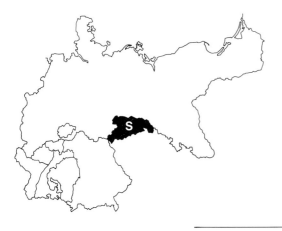

Garde-Reiter-Regiment. Armed as noted. Typical mark: 'G.R.R.2.35.' — 2nd squadron, weapon number 35.
Wachtmeister: P 08 and GROD
Vizewachtmeister: same
Fähnriche: P 08 and GRS
Trompeter: same
Hilfstrompeter: same
Sergeanten: P 08, GRS and lance
Unteroffiziere: same
Sanitätsmannschaften: P 08, and GROD or GRS

Karabiner-Regiment. Armed as Garde-Reiter, but officers, Wachtmeister and Vizewachtmeister carried distinctive degens rather than sabres; the other ranks were issued with cavalry sabres. Typical mark: 'K.2.25.' — 2nd squadron, weapon number 25.

Husaren-Regiment. Armed as Garde-Reiter (qv), but the distinctive 'state pattern' Kavallerie-Offizier-Säbel and Kavallerie-Säbel replaced the Garde-Reiter-Offizier-Degen and the Garde-Reiter-Säbel. Typical mark: '18.H.2.35.' — Königlich sächsisches 1. Husaren-Regiment König Albert Nr. 18, 2nd squadron, weapon number 35. Regiments concerned: 18 to 20, continuing the Prussian sequence.

Ulanen-Regiment. Armed as hussars (qv). Typical mark: '21.U.2.35.' — Königlich sächsisches 3.Ulanen-Regiment Nr. 21, Kaiser Wilhelm II, König von Preussen, 2nd squadron, weapon number 35. Regiments concerned: 17, 18 and 21 in the Prussian sequence.

Wurttbg

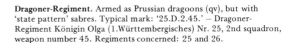

Dragoner-Regiment. Armed as Prussian dragoons (qv), but with 'state pattern' sabres. Typical mark: '25.D.2.45.' — Dragoner-Regiment Königin Olga (1.Württembergisches) Nr. 25, 2nd squadron, weapon number 45. Regiments concerned: 25 and 26.

Ulanen-Regiment. Armed as Prussian Ulanen (qv), but with 'state pattern' sabres. Typical mark: '20.U.3.15.' — Ulanen-Regiment König Wilhelm I (2.Württembergisches) Nr. 20, 3rd squadron, weapon number 15. Regiments concerned: 19 and 20.

Field artillery

Prussia

Garde-Feldartillerie-Regiment. Armed as regular field artillery regiments (qv). Typical mark: '1.G.A.4.25.' — 1.Garde-Feldartillerie-Regiment, 4th battery, weapon number 25. Regiments concerned: 1 to 4.

Feldartillerie-Regiment. Armed as noted. Typical mark: '15.A.r.2.25.' — 1.Ober-Elsässisches Feldartillerie-Regiment Nr. 15, 2nd mounted ('reitende') battery, weapon number 25. Regiments concerned: 1 to 11, 14 to 27, 30, 31, 33 to 47, 50 to 63, 66, 67, 69 to 76, and 79 to 84. In addition, the Lehr-Regiment der Feldartillerie-Schiess-Schule was similarly armed.
Wachtmeister: P 08 and AOS
Vizewachtmeister: same
Sanitätsvizefeldwebel: same
Unteroffiziere: P 08 and AS
Sanitätsunteroffiziere: same
Trompeter: same
Hilfstrompeter: same
Gemeine: same
Mannschaften zu Fuss: P 08 and S u/M
Note: many minor unit marks were associated with the field artillery, particularly the munitions columns or 'Munitionskolonnen'. Among these were: '1.M.I.52.10.' — light munitions column, I. Abteilung, 2.Ostpreussisches Feldartillerie-Regiment Nr. 52, weapon number 10; '1.F.M.II.52.10.' — light field howitzer ('Haubitz') munitions column, II.Abteilung, Feldartillerie-Regiment Nr. 52, weapon number 10; '1.M.4.K.D.10.' — light munitions column attached to 4.Kavallerie-Division, weapon number 10.

	Bavaria	The Bavarian field artillerymen carried the same weapons as their Prussian counterparts (qv), apart from the substitution of the Bavarian Artillerie-Seitengewehr M 92 for the u/M. Typical mark: 'B.3.A.2.50.' — 3.Bayerisches Feldartillerie-Regiment Prinz Leopold, 2nd battery, weapon number 50. Regiments concerned: 1 to 12.
	Saxony	The Saxon field artillerymen were armed in the same manner as the Prussians but carried Artillerie-Seitengewehre M 71 instead of the Seitengewehre u/M. Typical mark: as Prussia. Regiments concerned: 12, 28, 32, 48, 64, 68, 77 and 78 in the Prussian sequence.
	Wurttbg	Württemberg units carried the same weapons as the Prussians and Saxons, though a 'state pattern' Kavallerie-Offizier-Säbel replaced the Prussian Artillerie-Offizier-Säbel and a 'state pattern' Artillerie-Säbel was used. An Artillerie-Faschinenmesser replaced the Seitengewehr u/M. Typical mark: as Prussia. Regiments concerned: 13, 29, 49 and 65 in the Prussian sequence.

Foot artillery

	Prussia	**Garde-Fussartillerie-Regiment.** Armed as regular foot artillerymen (qv). Typical mark: 'G.A.F.2.65.' — 2nd battery, weapon number 65.
		Fussartillerie-Regiment. Armed as noted. Typical mark: '6.A.F.4.65.' — Fussartillerie-Regiment von Dieskau (Schlesisches) Nr. 6, 4th battery, weapon number 65. Regiments concerned: 1 to 11, 13 to 18, 20, and the Lehr-Regiment der Fussartillerie-Schiess-Schule. *Feldwebel: P 08 and AOS* *Vizefeldwebel: same* *Fahnenträger: P 08, and AOS or SfF* *Sanitätsvizefeldwebel: P 08 and AOS* *Sanitätsmannschaften: P 08 and S 98/05* Bespannungs-Abteilung *Wachtmeister: P 08 and AOS* *Vizewachtmeister: same* *Sergeanten: P 08 and AS* *Unteroffiziere: same* *Trompeter: same* *Gefreite: same* All units: *Einjährige-Freiwillige: P 08 and AS* Note: many minor units were attached to the foot artillery, particularly munitions columns or 'Munitionskolonne'.
	Bavaria	The state army had three foot artillery regiments in 1914, numbered from 1 to 3, and their weapons paralleled those of the Prussians — except that the Seitengewehr M 71 replaced the S 98/05.
	Saxony	The Saxon foot artillery regiments, numbers 12 and 19 in the Prussian sequence, were armed in identical fashion with the Prussian units. Typical mark: '12.A.F.3.25.' — 3rd battery, weapon number 25.
	Wurttbg	No foot artillery regiments.

Train

	Prussia	*Prior to an order of 19th March 1914, the Train-Abteilungen were known as Train-Bataillone, and the squadrons were referred to as 'companies'.*
		Garde-Train-Abteilung. Armed as regular units (qv). Typical mark: 'G.T.2.25.' — 2nd squadron, weapon number 25.
		Train-Abteilung. Armed as noted. Typical mark: '9.T.3.25.' — Schleswig-Holstein'sches Train-Abteilung Nr. 9, 3rd squadron, weapon number 25. Units concerned: 1 to 11, 14 to 18. *Wachtmeister, Vizewachtmeister and Sanitätsvizefeldwebel: P 08 and KOS. Sanitätsmannschaften: P 08 and KS.*

TABLE TEN 6

Note: there were many minor train markings, including: '9.T.B.2.25.' — Feld-Bäckerei-Kolonne (field bakery column) Nr. 2, attached to Train-Abteilung Nr. 9, weapon number 25; '9.T.F.3.25.' — Fuhrpark-Kolonne (transport or park column) Nr. 3, otherwise as before; '9.T.L.3.25.' — Feldlazarett (field hospital) Nr. 3, otherwise as before; '9.T.P.3.25.' — Proviant-Kolonne (supply column) Nr. 3, otherwise as before; '9.T.P.D.1.25.' — Pferde-Depot (horse depot) Nr. 1, otherwise as before; and '9.T.S.3.25.' — 3.Sanitäts-Kompagnie, Train-Abteilung Nr. 9, weapon number 25. Units raised in Hessen and Mecklenburg were armed in similar fashion with the Prussians, but carried distinctive 'state pattern' swords.

Bavaria

Train-Abteilung. Armed as noted. Typical mark: 'B.2.T.2.20.' — 2.Bayerische Train-Abteilung, 2nd squadron, weapon number 20. Units concerned: 1 to 3.
Wachtmeister: P 08 and AOS
Vizewachtmeister: same
Sanitätsvizefeldwebel: same
Sanitätsmannschaften: P 08 and KS a/A
Unteroffiziere: P 08 and IS 38
Gefreite: same
Gemeine: same

Saxony

Train-Abteilung. Armed as noted. Typical mark: '19.T.2.25.' — Königlich sächsisches 2.Train-Abteilung Nr. 19, 2nd squadron, weapon number 25. Units concerned: 12 and 19 in the Prussian sequence.
Wachtmeister, Vizewachtmeister and Sanitätsvizefeldwebel: P 08 and TOS. Sanitätsmannschaften: P 08 and AS.

Wurttbg

Train-Abteilung. The single Württemberg unit, number 13 in the regular series, was armed with the same weapons as the Prussians, but had its own regional sword and sabre variations. Typical mark: '13.T.2.25.' — 2nd company, weapon number 25.

Miscellaneous

Eisenbahntruppen (railway troops). Armed as noted. Typical marks included: 'E.2.85.' — Eisenbahn-Baukompagnie (railway construction company) Nr. 2, weapon number 85; 'E.A.2.85.' — Eisenbahn-Arbeiter-Kompagnie (railway work company) Nr. 2, weapon number 85; 'E.B.2.85.' — Eisenbahn-Betriebskompagnie (railway operating company) Nr. 2, weapon number 85; 'E.D.1.25.' — Militär-Eisenbahndirektion (military railway control unit) Nr. 1, weapon number 25. Units concerned: Eisenbahn-Regimenter Nr. 1 to Nr. 3, Eisenbahn-Bataillon Nr. 4, Bayerisches Eisenbahn-Bataillon.
Feldwebel: P 08, and IOD or IOS (AOS in Bavaria)
Vizefeldwebel: same

Telegraphentruppen (telegraph and field telephone units). Armed as noted. Typical marks included: 'A.𝔗.A.2.25.' — Armee-Telegraphen-Abteilung Nr. 2, weapon number 25; '𝔉.A.III.25.' — Fernsprech-Abteilung (field telephone unit) des III.Armeekorps, weapon number 25; '𝔉.A.G.25.' — Fernsprech-Abteilung des Gardekorps, weapon number 25; and '𝔗.A.G.25.' — Telegraphen-Abteilung des Gardekorps, weapon number 25. Note that the script 'T' was written as 𝔗 in Prussia, Saxony and Württemberg, but as 𝔗 in Bavaria. Units concerned: Telegraphen-Bataillone Nr. 1 to Nr. 6, and Nr. 8 (Prussia), Nr. 7 (Saxon), 1. and 2.Bayerisches Telegraphen-Bataillone, Festungs-Fernsprech-Kompagnie Nr. 1 to Nr. 6, and Nr. 8 (Prussian), Nr. 7 (Saxon).
Feldwebel: P 08, and IOD or IOS (AOS in Bavaria)
Vizefeldwebel: same
Fähnriche: P 08 and AS
Sergeanten: same
Unteroffiziere: same
Einjährige-Freiwillige: same

TABLE TEN **7**

Funker-Kompagnie (typical mark: 'F.T.A.1.25.' — Funkentele-graphen-Abteilung, or 'radio-telegraph unit', Nr. 1, weapon number 25).
Wachtmeister: P 08 and AOS
Vizewachtmeister: same
Fähnriche: P 08 and AS
Sergeanten: same
Unteroffiziere: same
Einjährige-Freiwillige: same

Luftschiffertruppen (airship units). Armed as noted. Typical markings included: 'L.A.1.15.' — Feld-Luftschiffer-Abteilung Nr. 1, weapon number 15; and 'L.L.1.15.' — Feldtrupp für Lenkluftschiffe Nr. 1, weapon number 15. Units concerned: Luftschiffer-Bataillone Nr. 1 to Nr. 5, and the Bayerische Luft- und Kraftfahr-Bataillon.
Feldwebel: as infantry regiments (qv)
Vizefeldwebel: same
Bespannungs-Abteilungen
Wachtmeister: P 08 and AOS
Vizewachtmeister: P 08 and AS

Fliegertruppe (aviation units). Armed as noted. Units concerned: Flieger-Bataillone Nr. 1 to Nr. 4, and the Bayerische Flieger-Bataillon.
Feldwebel: as infantry regiments (qv)
Vizefeldwebel: same
Sanitätsvizefeldwebel: same
Sergeanten: P 08 and KS 98
Unteroffiziere: same
Gefreite: same
Pioniere: same
Mannschaften: same

TABLE TEN **8**